James Endredy carries the old tradition of sacred storyteller, which he shares in a masterful way in his new book. His writing takes you into his experience so you feel a part of what he speaks, what he feels, what he learns about and sees. He offers down-to-earth explanations of the medicine ways so readers can apply the practical teachings in their own lives. It is a good time to sit down in a quiet place and open to what James Endredy's writing can bring into your awareness: the wisdom of respect for the sacred mystery of life and all its creations, seen and unseen, which is precisely what we need more of during these challenging times of transition. Read and enjoy, learn and grow, share with your friends, and live a good life. This book will help you on your road.

—Dr. Tom Pinkson, author, *The Shamanic Wisdom of
the Huichol: Medicine Teachings for Modern Times*

Lightning in My Blood is an extraordinary accomplishment, a powerful book of wonderful tales from James Endredy's life experience. Not only is he a compelling storyteller, but he is able to convey a great deal of useful information about the shamanic path through his magical tales. I highly recommend this book, both for the sheer fun of his humorous, harrowing stories and for its ability to carry you deeply into the world of the shaman.

—José Luis Stevens, PhD, author of *Praying with Power*

Be forewarned: when you open this book, you step into a different world, a world of cosmic clowns and dwarf kings, of water spirits and blue deer. As Endredy writes, "the shaman takes the first step of his journey where most take their last," and here the journey of the traveler begins and doesn't end until our dream of reality becomes the reality of our dreams. Nervous? Don't be. Actually, do be nervous. But dive in anyway.

—Hillary S. Webb, author of *Traveling Between the
Worlds: Conversations with Contemporary Shamans*

Lightning in my Blood

A Journey into Shamanic Healing
& the Supernatural

About the Author

James Endredy is a teacher, mentor, and guide to thousands of people through his books and workshops. After a series of life tragedies and mystical experiences as a teenager, he changed direction from his Catholic upbringing and embarked on a lifelong spiritual journey to encounter the mysteries of life and death and why we are all here. For over twenty-five years, he has learned shamanic practices from all over the globe while also studying with kawiteros, lamas, siddhas, roadmen, and leaders in the modern fields of ecopsychology, bioregionalism, and sustainable living. James also worked for ten years with Mexican shamanic researcher Victor Sanchez, learning to share shamanic practices with modern people.

On a daily level, his experiences have inspired him to live a sustainable lifestyle as much as possible while still working within mainstream society. He writes, leads workshops, mentors private clients, visits schools and community centers, speaks at bookstores, and volunteers in his community. His books—including *Ecoshamanism* and *Beyond 2012*—have thus far been published in seven languages.

Lightning in my Blood

A Journey into Shamanic Healing & the Supernatural

James Endredy

Llewellyn Publications
WOODBURY, MINNESOTA

FIRST EDITION
First Printing, 2011

Book design by Rebecca Zins
Cover design by Adrienne W. Zimiga
Cover image by Eric Williams/Koralik and Associates
Interior silhouette from Birds of a Feather font, www.iconian.com

Llewellyn is a registered trademark of Llewellyn Worldwide Ltd.

Library of Congress Cataloging-in-Publication Data
Endredy, James.
 Lightning in my blood: a journey into shamanic healing & the supernatural / James Endredy.—1st ed.
   p. cm.
 ISBN 978-0-7387-2147-7
 1. Shamanism. 2. Spiritual healing. 3. Supernatural. I. Title.
 BF1611.E655 2011
 201'.44—dc22

                                        2010049752

Llewellyn Publications
A Division of Llewellyn Worldwide Ltd.
2143 Wooddale Drive
Woodbury, MN 55125-2989
www.llewellyn.com

Printed in the United States of America

Contents

———— • ————

Acknowledgments

I must first express my gratitude to the folks at Llewellyn for their continued support, especially my long-time editor Rebecca Zins, Carrie Obry, publicist Steven Pomije, Amy Martin, and publisher Bill Krause. Special thanks to Ashley Becker and Benton Rooks for editorial assistance during the preparation of this book. Then I must acknowledge the many friends and colleagues who have been helpful and supportive during the course of this project: Marissa Joilette, Amy Gerber, Judy Bettencourt, Shawn Tassone, Kathryn Landherr, Eva Svingen, Valerie Wilsgard, Rahelio, Lupa, Jane D., Cody, Kate, Calib, Patricia, the family Calvitti, the family Endredy (Irma, Cindy, Kira, and Mike), Paul K., Tomas Pinkson, José Stevens, Hillary Webb, Sophie, and El Gato Bandito, to name a few. Finally, I am grateful to all of those, named and unnamed, who were part of these stories and who have graced my life. Thank you.

Lightning in My Blood

---·•·---

Once, in Q'ero, Peru, I had the privilege to spend many days with a very powerful and revered shaman/healer. During my second day with the old but vibrant man, he sat me down in a chair opposite the one he was sitting in. It was a beautiful, sunny day, and we were sitting outside in the shade of a large tree.

He said he needed to read the lightning in my blood to determine if we should continue working together. I was willing to accept his request. He leaned over to me and, using his hands, began taking my "pulse" at various parts of my body; mostly he concentrated on my temples, biceps, wrists, and calves.

After a half-hour or so, he began telling me things about my life he could not possibly have known or heard from someone else. Some of the things he told me about myself I had never even shared with another person. I was amazed, to say the least.

Then he began to divine my future, telling me things that would happen to me. Most of them have turned out to be true. When I asked him about how he reads the lightning in the blood, he told me, "When I was a young man I was riding my *paso* (Peruvian horse) through a field, and lightning came down and killed my horse. I was injured also by the lightning. I was ill for more than a year and had to be seen by a healer every day to keep my soul from leaving me. When I finally got better, the healer told me I must train to become a *curandero* (shaman/healer), because now I had the power of the lightning in my blood extra strong. Everyone has lightning in the blood, and that is why I can know what they need to be healed when I read them. But some people have more lightning than others. People with only a little lightning I sometimes have to read by touching them and then reading my own pulse because their lightning is too weak to read.

"It was very easy for me to read you, James, because even though you have not been struck by lightning, you have it strong in your blood from your ancestors—who were powerful medicine people of the Magyars—and from all the powerful places in nature you have traveled, the medicine teachers who have taught you, and the sacred plants you have eaten. You are not ready just yet to learn to read the lightning of other people. But you have many other important tasks the *apus* (mountain spirits) have given you. The blood in your left calf muscles told me that.

"I have one question for you, son. Why do you resist using your power and knowledge? Why are you reluctant? Now is your time, my son. The end of this world is less than ten years away, then comes a new epoch for humanity. You have been given the task to be an usher for people into this new stage. It is time for you to own your power, to set free the lightning in your blood!"

As the old curandero was speaking to me, many important moments in my life flashed before my eyes. These are the stories of some of those moments, both before and after that day, that the spirits have asked me to share with you...

Introduction

This is a book of my stories that delves into the world of shamanism. The stories come from the experiences throughout my life with hundreds of indigenous shamans, healers, and medicine people from over fifteen different specific cultures in South and North America, including Mexico and Hawaii. Although these cultures do not hold all or every specific shamanic tradition, practice, ceremony, or ritual throughout the globe, the lessons and teachings from this broad spectrum of remarkable people convey a vast range of knowledge that I hope will educate, inspire, and sometimes even awe or humor you, for that is what they have done for me.

The stories range from my somewhat wild teenage years when I first learned about spirits, energy, and tradition, to my later stories of sometimes brutal initiations and working with plant entheogens such as peyote, datura, san pedro, ayahuasca, and psylocibic mushrooms. Filled with the adventure of walking in the footsteps and being taught by who I consider to be some of the most powerful and knowledgeable people on the planet, these stories are a true journey into the supernatural.

My teachers, however, would not use the term *supernatural* at all. What they do is perfectly natural to them. As bizarre as some of the stories may seem, including seeing someone's future in a pool of blood, being healed by a guinea pig, being poisoned by datura, being chased by an evil witch who wanted to steal my soul, becoming psychically one with the earth while facing my death, being blessed by lizard blood, talking with animals, conversing with spirits such as an ancient dwarf-king, and learning to dream with the lords of the underworld, among many others, these types of experiences are what make a shaman.

However, shaman or not, the lessons are cross-cultural. The concepts and teachings in these stories related to the interconnection of all life, alternative healing methods, being able to laugh at yourself, respecting and learning from nature and her children, and simply opening up the rational mind to expand consciousness and experience new ways of looking at life and death are all lessons that can be applied by anyone in any culture.

For example, let's look at a short piece of an ancient parable by a famous Greek philosopher that may shed light onto the function and world of the shaman:

What if we were born and raised as prisoners in a dark cave? We stare at the cave walls and the images of shadows cast upon the walls. The shadows on the walls are of objects (people, animals, things) behind us that we cannot see but that are lit by a great fire that we also cannot directly see because our captors have chained us, preventing us from ever turning around. And so, as the years go by, our reality of the world is formed by the reality of the shadows. We know of nothing else.

But what if someone were to find a way to break free? With enough courage, he (or she) might eventually discover the objects making the shadows and also behold the fire.

If he were to finally find a way out of the cave, he would behold the sun, and eventually, as his eyes adjusted to the brightness, he would find himself in an alternate reality and would eventually become acclimated to this new world of light and form.

Upon returning to the cave with his knowledge of the world of light and the illusion of the shadows, many of the people in the cave would not believe his far-fetched stories. He would feel forlorn, but his undeniable experiences in the world of light would compel him to help cure the people of their myopia, to set them free into the light and demonstrate to them the nature of their shadow world. But would the people in the cave ever be open to adjusting their view of the world—the only world they have ever known?

This brief summary of Plato's famous "Allegory of the Cave," a parable concerning the way in which we understand the world, continues as he asserts that "if any one (in the cave) tried to loose another and lead him to the light, let them only catch the offender, and they would put him to death."

The prisoners in Plato's cave are ordinary men and women like me and you. Fortunately, there are those of us not satisfied with one consensus of reality, so we turn our heads and even try to get out from the cave to see the possibilities of other worlds. But today the situation is even more difficult than Plato's parable, written in 380 BC, because there are some who now even control the fire, the projector of mass images, and finally what we see in order to control us. Some of us escape our chains but, upon turning around and walking away from the shadows on the cave wall, we become entranced by the projector itself or want to be part of controlling it and therefore never make it out of the cave and into the light.

The principles contained in Plato's allegoric parable and the analysis of its philosophical implications can shed light onto the mysterious and often misunderstood subject of shamanism. It could be said that the earliest medicine men and women of prehistoric times—those that carried "otherworldly" knowledge, the shamans—were those who first turned around from the cave wall and took the light of the fire, exposing the source of the shadows and eventually walking in the light of a free consciousness.

Could Plato's parable then also be a metaphor for a shaman entering a trance state of higher awareness and perception? Or a shaman learning to use and control the mysterious consciousness of dreams? Or a medicine man summoning the spirit world? Is not the vast majority of modern Western culture currently basing its view of the world upon limited sensory perceptions and projections of media similar to the allegory of the people in the cave? Has our science, organized religion, and materialistic culture not killed or destroyed almost all of the "abnormal" tribal societies that did not conform to our rational, objective, anthropocentric worldview?

Due to the seemingly bizarre and misunderstood actions of shamans, "civilized" psychologists originally labeled them as deranged or schizophrenic; biologists viewed them as museum pieces of evolutionary history; sociologists categorized them as cultural anomalies; missionaries saw them as emissaries of the devil; and military leaders considered them completely inconsequential. However, even downplayed to the point of barely being human, shamans and medicine men continued to fascinate "civilized" people, and in the last few decades, the interest in shamanism has risen exponentially, as has interest in occult studies, the paranormal, and folk "magic" in general.

Although still a vast minority of the human population worldwide, there is undoubtedly a rising movement in Western cultures toward more sustainable lifestyles and a holistic worldview, as more and more people realize that many of the crises we now face have arisen from our anthropocentric worldview. Congruent with this paradigm shift, many people are seeking answers and inspiration from ancient tribal cultures that have lived (and in some cases still do live) in harmony and balance with each other and their environment. For most if not all of these tribes, it is the medicine man or medicine woman, the shaman, who is responsible for creating, maintaining, and correcting this balance and harmony. One of the most important roles of a shaman that is not widely acknowledged by modern seekers of shamanic knowledge is simply keeping the esoteric traditions of the tribe alive.

For tribes with no written language, the oral traditions—the stories and myths of the tribe—are of supreme importance, and the accurate narration of these stories becomes a sacred act. Those individuals who can recount them are held in the highest esteem. For example, there are Huichol shamans I know that can retell literally thousands of complex stories and myths from their tribe's history, and for many cultures not only is the learning of the stories a prerequisite for even being a shaman, the more stories a shaman knows—and his or her effectiveness in retelling them—has considerable implications on the shaman's status and reputation.

But whether a culture has a written language or not, everyone likes a good story. Stories give voice to our dreams, hopes, emotions, and creative thought. They have the power to pass on information and nurture collective memory (history). Stories tell where we've been and where we're going; they educate, transfer knowledge and traditions, and communicate cultural customs, social structure, and expectations of behavior. And, of course, they can entertain and amuse. In short, our stories explain our world.

The book of stories you are now holding came as a result of writing my previous book *Shamanism for Beginners: Walking with the World's Healers of Earth and Sky* (Llewellyn, 2009). While writing that book, I wanted to include quotes and stories from actual tribal shamans, something I found lacking in most other books on shamanism, and I also included a few of my own stories of walking in the shamanic world. During the creation of that book, my editors loved the stories and quotes from the tribal shamans, but they asked me to include more of my own stories, as they felt that readers would enjoy and benefit from them. It was then I realized, while recounting some of my own, that I had so many stories that an entire book could be filled with them. And so this book was born.

However, from the very first moments of starting this book, I realized it would lack power and the stories would not convey the actual shamanic experiences of non-ordinary reality if I wrote it with my purely rational mind. Nonfiction writing is accomplished primarily through memory and research. We learn something new and we write it down; we experience something new and we write it down. We remember what happened, whether it was just now or some time ago, and that forms the basis of our words that describe the event(s). However, our memory is not exactly the most reliable source of information. Our individual perception, point of view, cultural perspective, and state of mind, among countless other variables, ultimately affect what it is we actually remember about events that happen to us. This is why many people can have various recollections about the same event.

We all have individual "filters" that our experiences pass through before they become actual memories. But what if we could experience the moments and events of our life without our filters, without the controlling aspects of our ego, without defense or attachment? What if we were a clear vessel or lens that experiences could shine through without distortion, bias, or judgment?

Many Mesoamerican cultures that I have lived with make ceramic or wooden masks that depict or actually come apart into many different faces in succession behind the first face. The first face is the one through which we habitually see the world. But there are many faces behind this face. These are the faces that see beyond or behind our purely rational thoughts and perceptions. While the first face stares habitually at the cave wall, the other faces turn to look around, behind, underneath, over...

The first face tends to question or disbelieve such things as out-of-body experiences, travel to multi-dimensional realities, healing with crystals, speaking with animals, and most other forms of "paranormal" activities that are quite common in the world of a shaman. My stories included in this book come from the faces behind the first face. They invite us to explore and expand our view of reality and time and space.

The stories in this book are all "true" in the sense that they have been written from when I was in an altered state of consciousness, and the memories recounted come from the faces behind the face. Most of the stories do not run in chronological order, nor do they need to be read in order. There is no straight path on the journey of becoming or working as a shaman. The path weaves through time and space; it twists and turns between ordinary and non-ordinary states of awareness and perception.

I have been graced with life experiences that some people may find hard to believe, and I have learned from shamans so powerful that the results of their teachings have at times required me to seriously question my own sanity. But that is the way of the shaman. The shaman takes the first step of his journey where most others take their last. That's what shamans do. They learn to bend time and space and to walk in separate realities at the same time. It is not my concern or desire to convince you that my stories are true. My goal is to share with you some of what has happened to me in forty-something years on the shaman's path so that you may simply gain another perspective on this amazing tradition called shamanism.

Ted Williams, a Tuscarora medicine man, writes in his book *Big Medicine from Six Nations*, "Now of course this is too much. Some things shouldn't be told because people will think you're lying. Like when I put a quarter each into three different one-armed bandits at the Sahara in Las Vegas and hit a jackpot on each one."

With so many books that deal with the subject of shamanism from an anthropological point of view, all the way through to the plethora of books now available that cater to a lucrative New Age market and so restrict the content to the normal and accepted stories of shamanism, in the spirit of modern medicine men such as Ted Williams, Mad Bear, Joseph Marshall, Martín Prechtel, and Hosteen Klah, and modern healers employing the powers of story in their work such as Lewis Mehl-Madrona, Rita Charon, Arthur Frank, and Jesse Wolf Hardin, I offer some of my personal stories that I hope may broaden your scope of the topic. The cast of "characters" in this book include indigenous medicine men, medicine women, and shamans from tribes such as the Huichol, Seneca, Lenni Lenape, Apurímac Inca, Arapaho, Minnecojou Sioux, Kanaka Maoli, Tuscarora, Tukano (Columbia), Mazatec, Yurok, Navajo, Hopi, and Yucatec Maya. With this wide assortment of characters and their broad scope of associated lessons and teachings, the arrangement of the stories in this book was not an easy task.

However, there was a need for some form of structure, so I have divided the stories into chapters around the concept of medicine. "Medicine," in the shamanic world, is not the taking of a pill. Medicine can be anything that promotes healing, enhanced awareness, and increased perception, such as ceremony or ritual, the sunshine, a plant or animal, a sacred site, an initiation, dreamtime, and yes, even a story…

Medicine teachings of the sacred and mundane, light and shadow, blood and breath, life and death—all begin with experience. We don't have to be hit by lightning, bit by a snake, fall from a cliff, nearly drown in the ocean, be poisoned by a plant, psychically die, or be haunted by nightmares to learn about the shamanic term for medicine—but it sure helps.

Many blessings on YOUR journey!

James Endredy
SEDONA, ARIZONA
JANUARY 2010

Standing on the bare ground—my head bathed by
the blithe air and uplifted into infinite space—all
mean egotism vanishes. I become a transparent
eyeball; I am nothing; I see all; the currents of the
Universal Being circulate through me; I am part
or parcel of God.
RALPH WALDO EMERSON

CHAPTER 1
The Early Years:
The Medicine Teachings Begin

To truly know something is to experience it, just as Emerson actually experienced his relationship to God. In terms of shamanism, that's the bottom line, and that's why authentic shamans around the globe are put, intentionally or not, into experiences that invariably enhance their awareness and perception. To gain the medicine of sacred initiations, plants, animals, spirits, places of power, visions, stories, dreams, suffering, joy, fire, water, wind, and soil, a shaman is placed in a lifelong quest for experiences that transmit these medicine teachings so that he or she knows firsthand how they can be applied.

Space allows me to share only a small fraction of my medicine stories here in this book. My personal experiences with what many people would consider the paranormal or mystical began as a child, mainly with the forces of nature and medicine teachings of animals and trees during my elementary school years. In my early teens, my best friend and mentor, my father, died of brain cancer, and that experience set me off into a whole new realm of medicine teachings. My stories here begin shortly after the death of my father and what I consider to be the time period when I actually began to realize just how magical, mysterious, and tenuous life can be.

The Whispering of the Spirits

Sitting in the principal's office waiting for him to come in, I was shocked when, instead of the principal, an old Native American guy walked in and sat behind the principal's desk. My first impression of the man was that he looked like photos I'd seen of Geronimo, the Apache medicine man and war chief. He had dark, weathered skin and flowing white hair. His appearance was as fierce as a warrior, and he seemed hardened by a lifetime of living in the rugged outdoors—except this guy was wearing an impeccably tailored dark gray suit, with a white shirt and a black tie that matched his coal-colored eyes. He sat perfectly straight in the chair, with a calm but deadly serious look on his face, as he silently stared directly at me.

I started to ask him just what in the heck was going on, but he stopped me short with the raise of his hand and told me it was better to listen than to talk. He told me that his name was Matziwa, that he was a shaman, and that the whispering of the spirits had told him to come see me. Being in the eleventh grade and not having much knowledge about Native Americans, I really had no idea what a shaman even was.

He said he was there because one day I too might become a shaman, and he proceeded to tell me things about my life that he couldn't possibly have known. For the next fifteen minutes, I listened to the old man in an almost complete state of panic. His presence was so strong that I was immobilized and just sat there. He told me that I was at a crossroads in my life and that he was there to help me.

Matziwa then handed me a small, round mirror about three inches in diameter. The mirror was attached to a thin stick of hardwood, which acted like a handle so I could hold the stick and look into the mirror.

"The world we live in is a vast place full of mysteries and powers," Matziwa said. "But oftentimes we get trapped in our own little world to such a degree that we become isolated so that we can't see the bigger picture. Our problems, our victories, our desires—all seem so important that we easily forget we are all part of a much bigger reality. By looking into the mirror, you will be able to see yourself and the world at the same time. Use the mirror to see that you are indeed part of the mysterious world that surrounds you. Until you are well acquainted with the mirror, it is best to only use it when you are outdoors—that way, the mirror will reflect to you the natural world, the world of mystery and the unknown, instead of the world of strictly human affairs, the world of the known.

"The mirror is your first tool; it is an awareness-raising tool, and it can help open doors for you to different kinds of communication," he continued. "There will be many other tools and teachers that will cross your path. It is your responsibility to have your eyes and ears open when they come to you, so that you don't miss them and the lessons they have to share."

Just then the office door swung open loudly, and I turned around to see the large form of Principal Whittle entering the room with a scowl on his face. "Mr. Endredy," he started off sarcastically. "It's 8:35, which means that you're five minutes late. But judging from all these teacher reports I've received concerning your absence and tardiness, I'm not in the least surprised."

Principal Whittle proceeded to read off all the current charges against me, but I barely heard one word of what he was saying. I was in total shock, looking at the clock on the wall and wondering where in the hell Matziwa had gone. I had turned my head for just a second when Principal Whittle walked through the door, but by the time he had gotten to his desk, Matziwa had vanished. But by far the strangest thing was that according to the clock, my conversation with Matziwa had never happened. We had been talking for what seemed to be at least fifteen minutes, but that was impossible because it was still only 8:35. I was starting to wonder if I had gone completely nuts or if maybe I had just fallen asleep for a few seconds and dreamt the whole conversation with Matziwa.

I came back to my senses just in time to hear Principal Whittle suspend me from school for two weeks for skipping class. I almost laughed at the punishment, and the thought occurred to me to actually shake his hand and say thanks, but luckily I thought better of it. I got up from the chair and left Principal Whittle's office not knowing if I should feel happy or guilty about what had just happened. Suddenly I realized I was still holding the mirror on a stick. The mirror! So I wasn't hallucinating, and I couldn't have just dreamed the old man. Matziwa really had given me the mirror; the proof was in my hands.

Walking out of the school and to my car, I felt totally lost as to what to do next. I left the parking lot and started driving without thinking of where I was going. The next thing I knew, I was parked on the dirt road next to the house I had grown up in. The house was on the outskirts of town and adjacent to a wilderness area of hundreds of acres of woods, meadows, and streams. I used to have trails all through the woods and meadows there when I was little, and even though my family had moved many years before, I still knew the area like the back of my hand.

I got out of the car and walked aimlessly for a while. The sun was bright but it was a cold and breezy day, so I headed toward an area of pine trees where I used to go as a kid. I knew the pines would be a good place out of the wind to sit and think. When I arrived at the pine forest, a deep feeling of melancholy took hold of me, and I almost started to cry. I realized that this was one of my favorite places in the world, but I hadn't been there in years. I found a favorite old tree and sat on the ground with my back resting against its trunk. Memories from my childhood flooded in as the pine trees gently swayed back and forth with the wind and the sunlight peeked through the shadows of the forest and danced on the ground around me.

Somehow or another, being in the pines gradually made me feel better, and I promised myself to come back there again the next time I was feeling lost and confused. I slouched down a little more on the ground to get comfortable, and just then I felt something poke me slightly in the ribs. I reached into my pocket and pulled out Matziwa's mirror on a stick.

I raised the mirror up and looked at myself in it. I looked awful. My eyes were all swollen and red. I looked like I hadn't slept in days, which was pretty close to the truth. "What a weird day this has been," I said to myself.

As I continued to look at myself in the mirror, I heard a fluttering noise from behind me, and without thinking I turned the mirror so that I could see the area of woods behind me. I moved the mirror up and down until I saw a small bird that had landed on a branch in a tree behind me. The little bird must have made the sound I had heard. I continued moving the mirror slowly this way and that while looking into it. The effect was amazing, and I realized immediately that I had never looked into a mirror in broad daylight in the middle of a forest before. It was a completely new experience.

For the next half hour or so, I explored the different perspectives obtained by the mirror and discovered that it was really quite fun looking around with it. One moment I would look into the mirror at my face, meeting my eyes in it. Then, if I rotated it slightly to the right or left, I could see part of my head and a lot of what was behind me. By rotating it even more, I could watch the whole view of what was behind me without including myself in the reflected image. These last two views were completely foreign to me because, except for using the rearview mirror when driving my car, the only reason I ever looked in a mirror was to comb my hair. But now that I was looking at the rest of the world through a mirror, it was as if I was looking through a different set of eyes—like I was standing outside of my own body, looking at the world and seeing myself from the outside. It was an incredible feeling and one that immediately made my problems somehow seem not so urgent.

The thing that was most amazing was that not only was the feeling of being outside of myself a visual experience, but I also felt it on an emotional and intellectual level. It was as if my thoughts were coming from somewhere other than my own mind—like what I was thinking and feeling wasn't limited to the way I usually felt about myself and my life.

The wind blew with a mighty gust, and the whole experience shifted. From what had been a visual and thinking/feeling experience, I now found myself also listening to the world from a place outside of myself. The sounds of the wind blowing through the pine trees around me gave the impression of lots of little voices talking all at once—but they were not human voices using human words. It was like the trees and the wind were whispering to each other and talking about the little birds and the sunshine, the pine needles and squirrels, and all the other things that were around me.

It was in that moment that I realized I wasn't alone. Looking through the mirror, I discovered that I was simply one small thing in the middle of the forest, in the middle of this huge world. I was just like everything else: not any better and not any worse. Just one thing, one little part. And with that discovery I knew that what I was hearing, seeing, feeling, and thinking was not originating from purely inside of me, it was also, at the same time, coming from all around me.

Then I remembered what Matziwa had said to me earlier that morning. He had said, "I am a shaman, and the whispering of the spirits sent me to you. The spirits have told me that one day you may become a shaman also."

"This is too weird," I thought to myself and put the mirror back in my jacket pocket. The whisperings of the spirits? Is that what I was hearing? What were these spirits, and where did they come from?

Just then a tiny snowflake landed on my nose, and a completely separate thought popped into my head. Tonight was Friday night, ski club night, and three whole buses loaded with kids from school would be leaving soon to go up to the mountain and ski. Sure, I was suspended from school, but they couldn't stop me from driving up there on my own and skiing with my friends...

———————◆———————

A Matter of Energy

Through the night, the sky dumped over a foot of fresh snow on the ski mountain, and I couldn't resist spending my Saturday swooshing through the fresh powder. I drove down the long, winding road out of the valley, and when I got to the highway I stopped for some gas and a cup of coffee before heading to the mountain. As I was driving, I noticed the mirror that Matziwa had given me was sitting upright on the passenger seat like it was going for a ride, and it was reflecting the sunlight in really cool patterns on the dashboard. I must have set it there yesterday, but I didn't recall putting it there. I turned off the highway and started on the back roads to get to the ski area. It was about a forty-five-minute drive, so I put on some music and settled comfortably into my seat. After about fifteen minutes, I passed a road sign that I didn't ever remember seeing before. There were lots of little back-country roads in the area, so it was possible that I had just overlooked it in the past. But it wasn't probable, and the name of the road immediately grabbed my attention: Whispering Valley Road.

"Why are all these things about whispers coming to me lately?" I asked myself. First Matziwa's cryptic remarks, then my experience with the voices of the wind and trees, and now this road that had seemingly come out of nowhere.

Since I wasn't in a hurry, I decided to turn around and see where the mysterious road led. I turned right on Whispering Valley Road, and after a few more turns on back-country roads, I found myself parked at a small turn-out beside a creek, and on the other side of the creek was the most amazing old-growth forest of pines that seemed to be calling me.

As I got out of my car to walk down to the creek, I stopped, startled to notice a large deer, a whitetail buck, standing on the other side of the creek, staring at me. I stood stone-still, not wanting to scare him away. He stared intently at me and I back at him. I was surprised that he didn't run away, and I continued down to the creek, expecting him to take off at any moment. But I got all the way down to the water, and he was still standing there nonchalantly looking my way. Very strange. That certainly wasn't normal for a whitetail buck in these parts. I wondered what he'd do if I crossed the creek, so I began hopping from one rock to another in order to cross without getting my feet soaked. As soon as I got to the other side of the creek, he trotted off. The weird thing was that he still wasn't running away, and I could swear if I didn't know better that he was trying to get me to follow him.

When I got to the place where I first saw the buck standing, I noticed that there was a trail leading into the woods, so I began to follow it. Soon I discovered that the trail was taking me exactly into the old-growth forest that I wanted to visit. It was incredible. The pines were enormous, and the feeling of the forest was even more magical than in my little spot I had visited the day before. Up ahead, I saw a small bench that someone had built out of pine branches and cleverly attached to the base of one of the largest trees. I couldn't resist trying it out, so I went over and sat down.

As I sat down, I felt the now-familiar poke of the mirror on a stick in my pocket, and I pulled it out. I didn't remember taking the mirror off the seat of my car and putting it into my jacket. I sat there in disbelief, looking at it in my hand, when I noticed the reflections it was giving off. I began to slowly look at the scenery with the mirror just as I had the day before, except this time I got into the feeling of being one with the forest much more quickly, and the beauty of the place seemed to be amplified by the mirror to such an extent that everything seemed to be shimmering, including the side of my head that I could see reflected in it.

I put the mirror down and gasped because I could still see everything shimmering, or faintly glowing, with a radiant light. On one side, the huge pine trees were shimmering as if covered with gold dust, and on the other side, as I looked down toward the creek, I saw the water and the plants and the other trees were shimmering with light as well. Then I saw the deer again, and he was glowing the most brightly of all—a clear and radiant blue color.

Suddenly I heard footsteps coming down the hill. Not knowing what to do, and figuring I was on private property, I hightailed it down to the stream bank and hid behind a large oak tree. I heard the footsteps drawing nearer, and they seemed to stop near the bench I had been sitting on. Darn! In my hurry, I had left the mirror sitting on the bench.

"Who's there?" a voice cried out.

The voice sounded familiar, but I couldn't place it. "Come on out, I know you're there. We don't care if people come to this place as long as they treat it respectfully. If you're not doing anything wrong, you've got no reason to hide."

Feeling rather silly for running, I came out from behind the tree and was completely shocked by who I saw. It was Amy, a girl who had accidentally run into me while skiing the day before. I had helped her after our crash, and we had enjoyed a brief but very interesting conversation. We had taken the lift back to the top of the mountain together, and for some reason I had ended up giving her a short synopsis of my life, including the fairly recent death of my father and some of the problems I was now dealing with in my life. I had felt an immediate attraction toward Amy that was much more than physical. Even in the short amount of time we had spent together during our first meeting, there was something about Amy that fascinated and intrigued me. She was extremely self-assured without being arrogant, she was articulate but not snooty, and she somehow had effortlessly drawn me into a conversation about myself without me even realizing it. When we had said goodbye at the top of the mountain, I had secretly hoped that we would meet again sometime.

"Well, well, well. Look who it is," she said with a friendly smile, not seeming the least bit surprised to see me. "If I didn't know better, I'd think you were following me, Jim Endredy."

"N—no. I wasn't, Amy, I swear," I stuttered, feeling totally embarrassed. "What are you doing way out here, anyway?" I asked, now feeling a bit defensive.

"This is my uncle's property. I live with him at his house at the top of the hill," she replied, pointing up into the forest behind us.

"Wow, this is too weird," I said as I tried to process the chances of actually arriving to where she lived by complete accident. "Talk about coincidences—I was just driving toward the ski area and saw this road and decided to see where it went. I never meant to come looking for you or anything like that, I swear."

"Come on over here and sit down. I think we need to talk," Amy said with an air of mystery.

She sat down on the bench and motioned for me to sit next to her. Much to my chagrin, she was holding my mirror in her hands, and she placed it in her lap as she sat down. I sat shyly next to her, and she began, "First of all, there are no coincidences. This is something that you're going to learn real quick on the path of the seer. Seers notice everything that crosses their path—they keep their eyes open and their ears sharp because they know that the Mystery is sending them messages all the time. From now on, you'd do best to forget about the word *coincidence* and look deeper into the meanings of the things and people that cross your path."

"Just what do you mean by 'seer'?" I asked hesitantly.

"Is this your mirror on a stick?" she asked with a smirk as she handed it back to me without answering my question.

"Well, yeah," I admitted.

"I'm guessing that you didn't make it in Boy Scouts, did you?" she asked knowingly and added, "It's all starting to make sense now."

"What's making sense? This whole thing is confusing the crap out of me," I said loudly, starting to feel irritated.

She let out a clear and melodious laugh that was both hearty and dainty at the same time. "You poor boy. You really have no idea what you're in for."

That set me off. "Now wait a minute, Amy. Who are you calling *boy*? You're only a year older than me, plus I've been across the country and back and have lived on my own. So don't give me this *boy* stuff. I want you to explain to me what makes sense in this whole business, right now!"

"You're sensitive—and defensive," she replied calmly. "But I guess that's to be expected after all you've been through. Okay; listen—I apologize for calling you a boy. I only said that because in terms of the path you are about to take, you are like a newborn child. You've just begun, whereas I, on the other hand, have been receiving instruction on becoming a seer since I was four years old. This isn't easy to explain, and I'm not the best person to do it, but it looks like it's my job to start you off.

"For seers," she continued, "everything is seen to happen for a reason. When you first start out on the path, coincidences seem to be random acts—like when you're thinking about someone and then the phone rings, and it's them calling. But once you begin to pay close attention to everything that is happening around you, these little coincidences start becoming more and more frequent. For a seer, this becomes like a snowball effect, and the coincidences happen so often that they aren't seen as coincidences anymore, they are simply a way of life. Some seers call it 'being in the flow,' because once you pay attention to all the messages that the coincidental events hold, you begin to flow with them from one to the next in a smooth and harmonious way. For example, when I ran smack into you on the ski slope yesterday, for me, since I'm a seer, I knew right away that that couldn't have been just a random event. No seer just runs into someone like that without there being a darn good reason. At the time, I didn't know what the reason was, but I knew I had to try to find out, and that's why I asked you about yourself on the chair lift. After we spoke, I still wasn't exactly sure why I had run into you, but I was sure that I would find out if I let things unfold naturally—and, well, here you are, and now I know why. It's because you've been put on the seer's path. You're one of us, even though you don't realize it yet."

"But what in the world is a seer?" I asked, still confused.

"Seers are people who can see the underlying magic in life because they have polished their connection to the world. Instead of struggling through life, they open themselves to the natural unfolding of life around them in every minute. This gives them a unique way of seeing the world. I'm guessing you've already had this type of experience. Why don't you tell me about your mirror?"

"This old Native American guy gave it to me," I replied. "But I'm not sure if he really even exists. He told me that it is a tool that shamans use. But I don't even know what a shaman is, and I'm not sure I want to. I've looked into the mirror a few times and saw some cool things."

"Can you explain what you saw?" she asked.

"Well, it's like when I look in the mirror, I can see myself and the world around me at the same time, instead of just looking at the world through my own eyes like I normally do. When I see myself and the world at the same time, I can see that I'm a part of the world, and that feeling separate and alone is just an illusion because we are never really separate or alone."

"Very good," she said with an open and friendly smile. "What else?"

"I don't know what to make of it," I replied, "but just before you came down the hill, I was looking into the reflection of the mirror, and I saw all the living beings in the forest were shimmering with light. Even after I put the mirror down, everything was still kind of glowing, especially a large buck that was standing down by the stream. But I don't see anything shimmering here anymore."

"Wow, that's pretty impressive for a beginner," she said. "You've already begun to see the energy fields of living beings. Congratulations. In those moments when you were seeing the shimmering energy, the thoughts inside your head were quieted, and you were looking at the world without judgment. You were seeing the world as it truly is. The beauty and power of these ancient trees helped you to quiet your thoughts and expand your perception of the world. You don't see the world that way right now because since we began speaking together, your head has been filled with all kinds of thoughts. With more practice, you'll be able to see energy fields whenever you want to. That's one of the greatest gifts of seeing, because it allows you to see how the world is really working. But I'm sure you will find out more about that later, from someone better able to explain it than me. Seers have certain specialties, according to their energetic makeup and personality. I'm like my uncle; we're both wind—the communicators. Our specialty is receiving and delivering the messages of the spirits. That's why I said earlier that it was all making sense now. Since you're just starting on the path, you need guidance from someone who is an expert teacher, and that's why you were guided here. My uncle is going to be one of your teachers; he's not only a seer, he's a shaman—a shaman of the wind."

"There's that word again. So what is a shaman?"

"Shamans are seers that help to keep balance in the world. They are healers and teachers who have received a call from the spirits to serve. I haven't received my call yet, but I hope to one day."

"So how do you know your uncle's going to be my teacher?" I asked.

"He told me a few minutes ago," she replied. "Do you think I came down here and found you by accident? Hardly. He told me to come get you. He knew you were here as soon as you crossed the creek. He's connected to every living thing that lives and grows on this land, even the deer," she said, and she looked squarely at me with an intense look in her eyes.

As soon as she mentioned the deer, a chill ran down my spine. Now that I looked back on it, that big buck I had seen by the creek had been acting very strangely, and as I thought about it more, there was something very peculiar about its eyes. They looked almost human…

"Come on," she said and stood up, offering me her hand. I took it and stood up, facing her.

She looked into my eyes, and for some unknown reason I felt a peacefulness and happiness that I hadn't felt in long time—probably since my father had gotten sick two years before. I could smell a sweet fragrance from her as her hair blew slightly in the breeze. Her hand felt soft and smooth in mine, and her touch was gentle yet firm. I looked into the wells of her eyes, and in some inexplicable way I felt like I was home—like I had found something I really belonged to.

In that moment, I began to see her whole body sparkling with light. It was the most incredible thing I had ever seen and so beautiful I can't even describe it. All I can say is that my perception was dual. I could clearly see her smiling face and her body as she stood in front of me holding my hand, but at the same time I could see her as a glowing sphere of pure energy. I think it was the unconditional affection that I felt for her in that moment that opened me up to being able to see her in that way. My feelings for her weren't possessive, or sexual, or even romantic. They were simply pure feelings of affection, without desires or conditions.

I looked away from her eyes and saw the buck standing on the trail leading up the hill. It was glowing a deep blue. Amy looked up the hill and saw the buck too. Then she turned back to me and said, "It's time to go up."

Amy led me up the hill on a trail that ran in between the giant trees of the enchanted forest. We walked single file, without talking. When we reached the top of the hill, I saw a small house off to my right that was nestled in a grove of smaller trees and that looked out over a big garden and a cleared field. We continued walking a short distance down the trail, which was now running across the top of the ridge and still very much inside the forest of huge trees.

She stopped walking and abruptly turned to face me. Taking both of my hands in hers, she told me to look straight into her eyes. After I did, she instructed me to take a deep breath, clear my thoughts, and very slowly lift my head to look way up into the trees just behind her. I did as she said. At first all I saw were trees, then suddenly—almost as if by magic—my eyes really saw, and the wonderment took away my breath. High up in front of me was a gigantic tree house perched atop six huge trees. Upon first glance, it could have been missed by the casual observer. But once identified, it was easy to see how carefully it had been constructed to be one with the trees. It seemed to be a part of the forest, as if it had grown there from a seedling. Moving closer, I was struck by how it mirrored the trees supporting it. The main structure was round like a tree trunk and the stairs to enter it were cleverly concealed as a formation of vines circling upward. A deck jutted outward, surrounding the entire structure, weaving itself in and out of the trees, giving a final sense of unity between man-made and nature-created. Continuing to move forward, I noticed that the space between the top of the walls and the roof was open, and I watched as birds flew in and through the house. My intense amazement at this architectural wonder was suddenly jarred as a voice boomed from above, "Welcome, young seer! I am Humphrey. Come up, come up!"

My curiosity about what was inside didn't need much encouragement. Amy had been following me as I approached the tree house. I turned toward her, and she motioned me onward. With only a slight hesitation at going alone, I ascended the vinelike staircase, and when I reached the top, Humphrey greeted me by asking, "And what do they call you in the outside world?"

"My name is Jim, sir, or James—James Endredy."

"No need for sirs here, Jim," he replied. "Just call me Humphrey. Now, tell me: who sent you to me?"

"I don't understand, sir—I mean, Humphrey—no one sent me. I just found this place by accident."

Humphrey was a tall man with wind-blown, sandy hair, and he laughed loudly at my answer. I looked around the inside of the tree house, not believing what I was seeing. "Ha-ha-ha! No one just arrives here by accident, young man," he said as he bent forward to look straight into my eyes. "Let me ask the question in another way. Have you met anyone new lately whose eyes look like mine?"

Humphrey bent toward me even closer and looked me intensely in the eyes. Immediately, I saw the same sort of reflection in his eyes that I had seen in Matziwa's in the principal's office.

"Matziwa," I said as I glanced away. Humphrey stood up straight once again. His large presence seemed to engulf both me and the tree house with a powerful magnetic energy.

"Ah, I see," he said, as he kind of looked at me sideways. "Matziwa," he repeated very carefully. "Well, okay, that's good enough for me. We can talk about Matziwa later. Right now, we've got a lot to do and see. But first I want you to come and stand over here in the center so we can have a look at you."

He guided me to the very center of the round tree house, where directly above me was a large hatch in the roof that was open so that the sun was shining down on me. There were perches for birds on all four sides around me. Each perch was made of wood and was about four feet tall and about six feet from where I was standing. Humphrey walked around the tree house and closed all the windows with wooden shutters to block the light, except for four large windows that were at opposite sides of the tree house from each other.

"These four windows face the four cardinal directions," Humphrey explained. "The north, south, east, and west."

He then pointed to one of the windows. "I want you to turn and face that window, the window to the north."

I turned my body so that I stood facing the north window, and I could feel the warmth of the sunlight on the top of my head and shoulders from the open hatch in the center of the roof above me.

"Now all I want you to do is stand there for a few moments without feeling self-conscious or embarrassed or anything. Just take a few deep breaths, relax, and no matter what happens, just stay where you are, and everything will be fine," Humphrey explained very clearly as if he wanted to make sure that I understood. Then he walked around me and positioned himself next to the bird perch that was directly behind me.

After a few seconds of standing there waiting, Humphrey made a loud screeching call, and immediately a large bird—I thought it was an eagle—flew into the tree house, circled around a few times, and then landed on the perch next to Humphrey, behind me. I glanced over my shoulder and saw the eagle and Humphrey looking at each other, and I could have sworn that they were somehow talking to each other about me, but I couldn't hear what they were saying. I turned my head back to face the north window, and then Humphrey began to sing a strange song in a language I didn't understand. His voice started out very softly, but as he kept singing it got louder and louder until he was singing at full strength.

When his voice reached full volume, a strong wind began to blow in from the window directly in front of me—the window to the north. The air of the wind had a unique quality: it was cold and fresh. It felt like the wind blowing across newly fallen snow from high up on a mountain. The wind made me feel like I was standing at the top of a snow-covered mountain, looking out over the world.

I couldn't see this at the time, but I know now that Humphrey had extended his arms with his palms facing me, and the eagle had opened its wings wide. Both Humphrey and the eagle were "reading" the north wind as it came through the window and passed over my body.

After a few minutes, the wind stopped, and Humphrey told me to turn to the right and face the window of the east. As I turned, Humphrey and the eagle moved as well, and they positioned themselves in back of me once again. Humphrey began to sing, a wind began to blow through the window, and as his song got stronger, so did the wind.

The wind of the east was completely different than the wind from the north. It felt warmer, but not hot, and it definitely smelled like the ocean. I could actually taste the salt air, and if I closed my eyes I could easily imagine that I was standing on the beach with a breeze coming off the ocean blowing through my hair. I couldn't believe what I was feeling, but there was no denying it.

When the east wind stopped, I was instructed to face south, and Humphrey and the eagle followed the same routine. The wind began to blow at me through the south window.

The south wind was hot and dry. It felt like I was standing in the middle of a hot and inhospitable desert. It made my eyes burn slightly, and I almost had the impression that sand was blowing at me.

I was happy when the south wind ended, and I quickly turned to the final position, the west.

Humphrey began his song, and I could hear the eagle on the perch behind me. The west wind began to blow through the window, and I was surprised and happy to feel that it was a tranquil wind. It reminded me of a slight breeze blowing gently through an airy garden. I could actually pick out the fragrance of different flowers and fruit such as apples and pears. Then the smells changed to trees such as pine and cedar. And finally, just before the wind started to die down, I could clearly smell the smoke from a wood-burning fire.

As I continued to look out toward the window of the west, I could distinctly see tiny wisps of smoke coming in with the wind through the window. The bright sun combined with the smoke gave the illusion of a kind of smoky fog that eventually covered the whole window. An image seemed to be forming in the smoke, and I struggled to make out what it was. Gradually, I began to see a small fire, and there was a man sitting next to the fire looking straight into it and singing some words that I didn't understand. Just as the image came into clear view, the man looked up from the fire and turned his head to look directly at me. It was Matziwa!

Humphrey came and stood beside me to look at the window of the west with me. The image of Matziwa turned to look at Humphrey and said a few words to him that I couldn't make out, then Matziwa looked back at me and smiled as the image faded and the wind gently blew the smoke from the window.

"The winds of the four directions have told us a lot about you, James," Humphrey said as he walked toward a door on the south side and motioned for me to follow him.

We came out onto the deck that ran around the outside of the tree house, and we sat down on comfortable wooden chairs that faced south, overlooking the great forest.

"I imagine you must have a great many questions rolling around inside your head right now," Humphrey continued as he filled and handed me a glass of water from a pitcher that sat on a small table between us. "The world is changing, young man. And the four winds have shown me that you will be part of that change.

"Throughout the ages, there have been certain people called prophets and mystics. These special individuals had very intense spiritual experiences that they shared with the rest of people. The people then formed religions and spiritual groups around the visions of their prophets. But the time has now come for people to have their own personal visions and intensely spiritual experiences. This transformation from people following religions to discovering their own visions will take time, but there are already those who are doing it. These people are what we call seers, and they are growing in number every day.

"Seers come in many different forms and have many different specialties. But each seer gains their vision through connection to one or more of the great powers that rule the world: the wind, water, earth, fire, and the spirit that lives in all things. The wind seers are the communicators—their specialty is to receive and transmit information at many different levels.

The water seers are the shapeshifters—they have many talents and can easily flow from one job to the next. They keep things moving without asking a whole lot of questions. The earth seers are the creators—they are the grounded ones who build things and take care of them. They nurture the seeds of dreams and help them to grow and prosper. The fire seers are the visionaries—they are the passionate ones who are never really happy with the way things are, so they are constantly searching for new ways of seeing and doing things.

"All seers connect to the spirit that lives in all things, because it is what animates and gives life to the world. I am a wind seer, and the wind is my main ally. Because I am a wind seer, a communicator, I have been given the task to explain to you what is happening to you and to be a guide in your new role as a seer.

"The four winds have shown us that you are a fire seer. When you faced the west, which to you in this place is the direction of the fire, the west wind delivered a vision to you. That means that the fire is your ally in the same way that the wind is mine. Can you tell me what you saw in your vision?"

"In the window of the west I saw smoke, and then in the smoke I saw the old man, Matziwa, sitting by a fire," I replied.

"Yes, I saw him and the fire also," said Humphrey, smiling. "This tells us there is no doubt that you are a fire seer, as is Matziwa. Now that we know that, we can begin your training."

"My training?" I asked hesitantly.

"Of course!" replied Humphrey exuberantly. "Your training to become a seer—you already have the talent, but you need to learn how to use it. We will begin right away!"

Just then, Amy walked through the door on the deck and sat down to join us.

"He's fire," said Humphrey matter-of-factly to Amy.

"I had a feeling he was fire when I spoke with him yesterday and he told me some of the stories about his life. He's all over the place," Amy replied to Humphrey like I wasn't even sitting there.

"What do you mean, I'm all over the place?" I asked defensively. "You don't even know me!"

"But we know that you're fire and that you're having problems," Humphrey answered while looking intently at me. "It's nothing to be defensive about," he added reassuringly. "Fire seers are very passionate—you just need to learn how to use your fire in the proper way and to balance it with the other powers."

"I don't understand," I said, feeling very confused. "I still don't know what you mean about me being fire."

"Let's see if we can't clear this up for you," replied Humphrey, staring intently at me. Opening his eyes wide and raising his eyebrows, he said, "Tell me, what do you prefer doing more: going skiing or reading a book?"

"No question about it," I answered. "Skiing."

"Of course you like skiing more than reading. When you are skiing, you use your instincts, you move rapidly from one place to the next, your body reacts quicker than your mind, and your passion wins out over your thoughts. This is the fire, don't you see? It's the same for the other things you prefer to do, like rock climbing and surfing and skydiving. You'd much rather do those things than sit in school."

"That's right," Amy added. "As for me, if I had the choice between freezing my butt off going skiing, risking my life rock climbing, or sitting in a nice cozy room with a good book, I'd pick reading the book almost every time. That's because I'm wind—I'm a communicator. What I need is information, but you, on the other hand—what *you* need is passion."

"Let's give him another example," Humphrey said to Amy.

Turning to me again, Humphrey said, "I understand you lost your father last year. Let's look at what you did after that traumatic event. You escaped, didn't you? You left home to look for adventures. You went searching for things to feed your passion, to feed your fire. If you were wind, you would have sought counsel. But you didn't, because you hate counsel. If you were earth, you would have stayed grounded and used your home, family, and friends to support you in your time of need. But you didn't, because you can't stand staying at home. If you were water, you would have found a different way to channel your anger; you would have explored many different paths and outlets to ease the pain of your loss. But you didn't, because you're hot-headed and make immediate decisions based on your instincts."

"There's no doubt that you're fire," said Amy. "Can you see that now?"

"Now that you put it that way, I guess I can see what you mean," I replied. "But why relate everything to wind, water, earth, and fire?" I asked, still not completely convinced.

"Seers are very practical," Humphrey replied, "and the most practical and powerful way to relate to the world is to become allies with the forces and powers that rule the world. Most people think that human beings rule the world because we are the most intelligent. We can build or destroy great cities whenever we choose, and we have learned to harness the powers of the earth, wind, water, and fire to serve us. But this feeling of controlling the world with our mighty machines is merely an illusion. The powers of earth, wind, water, and fire were here billions of years before us, and they will still be here long after we are gone. The great powers don't need us, but we certainly depend on them. Do you realize what happens if we are without even one of the great powers? We die. The earth, wind, water, and fire provide us with life. We are them, and they are us. It's that simple. But most people have forgotten that, and that's why they don't see. For seers, working with the great powers is the most fundamental aspect of life."

"So you're saying that we are all earth, wind, water, and fire, but you call me fire because I have more fire in me than the others?" I asked.

"That's right," replied Humphrey. "And just like the powers of the world work in harmony to sustain life on the planet, so do we have to work together to live in balance and happiness with the powers. You represent the human heart of the fire, just like Amy and I represent the wind. Your task is to learn to be the fire in a way that creates harmony and happiness with the other powers and the people that represent the other powers. When you do that, you will not only be happy yourself, but you will make a positive contribution to the world."

"But why me, Humphrey?" I asked. "Why am I supposed to do this?"

"It's all a matter of energy," he replied.

"It's all a matter of energy," Amy repeated, nodding her head affirmatively.

Humphrey continued. "All the things we've been talking about can be boiled down to one thing: energy. The great powers of earth, water, wind, and fire provide us with vital energy, and when we learn to use that energy in a balanced way, we live healthy lives. But seers take it to the next level. When we learn to link our internal energy with the energy of the powers around us, we expand our energy to be informed about the world at a much greater level. That's what I did earlier when I put you into the energy of the wind. I connected with the wind in order to be informed at a much higher level than just by my own thoughts and judgments. Now, to answer your question: no one can know why we are chosen for our tasks in life. Why one person is good at writing and another is good at building things. How someone is talented at music and another person is an excellent teacher. All we can do is try as hard as we can to find our true task in life and then use our energy to accomplish it. Right now, your task is to become a seer of the fire and help restore balance to the world by representing the fire in the realm of human beings. You are extremely fortunate to have found your task at a young age. Many people live their whole life without ever knowing their true task in life. The question is—will you accept your destiny?"

"But this sounds so far out," I replied, looking out over the valley and trying to grasp what was happening to me.

"Of course it sounds strange," Humphrey answered. "The heroes of these days are movie stars and professional athletes, bankers and lawyers. Who ever heard of a famous seer? But that's the whole point. A great change needs to take place in the world, and it is beginning to happen right now. Human beings are out of balance; they are destroying the world with their massive cities and pollution of earth, water, and sky. The world doesn't need more millionaire actors or sports heroes; it doesn't need more polluted cities, automobile factories, or video games. What the world needs now are people who can see how to restore the balance between human beings and the world that gives us life."

"How do we see that?" I asked.

"The next step for you is to see the movement of energy," answered Humphrey. "You've already started to do that by using the mirror that Matziwa gave you. With the help of the mirror, you were able to see how you are an integral component of the world, not just a separate human being. Then, once you saw that, your perception of the world opened even further so that you saw the energy of the living beings around you. The way to perceive that energy is to see without judgments or thoughts about what you are looking at. In the beginning, this usually happens when you see the pure beauty of the things around you. Think about it: all of the things that you have so far witnessed as energy are things that your heart finds beautiful—the trees, the stream, the deer…and even Amy," he added with a knowing look and a raise of his eyebrows.

Amy blushed and quickly looked away from me as Humphrey continued. "The next step for you is to see how energy moves. For example, here in my hand I have a river rock that has been sitting in the shade. Right now it feels cool to the touch. But if I take the rock and put it in the sun, the rock will absorb the energy of the sun and get warmer. Then, when the sun sets, the rock will slowly cool by releasing the energy of the sun that it had collected into the air. This movement of energy between sun, rock, and air is easy to see and feel. The same movement of energy applies to everything in nature: between fire, water, sun, trees, flowers, fish, birds, and soil. But what most people don't realize is that a similar movement of energy takes place between people as well. Physically, emotionally, and psychically, we are constantly sending and receiving energy to and from everything around us. I want you to try to see the movement of this energy between people."

I was thrilled when Humphrey went on to tell me that from now on, I could use the tree house whenever I wanted, as long as I came alone. He and Amy lived in the small house at the top of hill, but the tree house was a place reserved especially for connecting with the wind and birds, and for studying and practicing seeing. Amy explained that Humphrey was a physics professor at a nearby university, where he usually taught classes in the mornings. He also was the founder of a rescue and rehabilitation center for injured and sick birds, so he spent most of his afternoons at the center.

Many of the birds that lived around the tree house had been treated and cared for by Humphrey at the center and then released into the area around the tree house, where many had stayed. She said that was one of the reasons why Humphrey knew all the birds here so well—they looked up to him like a father.

Humphrey became somewhat of a father figure to me as well. During the next few months, he helped me understand the link between the new paradigm of modern physics and the ways of ancient and current shamans and seers. Under his tutelage, I actually learned to enjoy reading and was astonished at how many books I read while at the tree house. Since Amy was also a communicator, she was constantly giving me books and striking up conversations about philosophical and esoteric subjects I had never even thought about before.

However, maybe the greatest gift Humphrey gave me was the task of caring for an injured eagle whose name was Ronnie. Somehow, the very first day I met the eagle at his clinic, Humphrey saw the special relationship that would eventually develop between Ronnie and myself. After a few weeks at the clinic, Humphrey let me bring Ronnie to the tree house to take care of him so our contact was almost daily. Ronnie the eagle was no normal being. In a similar way to Humphrey, Matziwa, and, to a certain extent, Amy, he was acutely aware of realities I could not yet even fathom. But at the level of feelings and emotions, he became (and in spirit still is) one of the greatest and most beloved friends I have ever had.

The Eagle's Gift

When Ronnie's wing was finally healed, I agreed to help Humphrey release him back into the wild. It broke my heart to think that I might never see Ronnie again, but now that he could fly I knew he'd be happier once he was free—I knew I would be if I were him.

We left at dawn to drive to the tallest mountain in the area, about an hour away. The road climbed higher and higher up the mountain until it ended in a small parking area about two-thirds of the way to the top. We'd have to walk the rest of the way to where we would release Ronnie.

We walked along a narrow path that climbed higher up the mountain through steep, rocky terrain until eventually we were higher than the trees and surrounded by bare rock near the top of the mountain. We carefully made our way a little higher and then traversed across the rocks until we came to a wide ledge at the top of a sheer cliff.

"This is the place where I bring eagles like Ronnie once they are healed," said Humphrey. "From here, they can fly high above the world and choose where they want to go next. Sometimes they find their way back to the tree house and live for periods of time there with me; other times, I never see them again. Since you helped Ronnie to get healthy and you two have become such close friends, I think it's appropriate for you to send him off on his journey."

Humphrey explained the procedure for me to follow. I put the leather protector on my arm, opened Ronnie's cage, and he jumped happily onto my forearm. He seemed to know exactly what was going on, and he flapped his wings a few times to stretch, then sat perfectly still on my arm while looking directly at me.

"I wish you all the best on your journey," I said to Ronnie in an emotional voice. "You've helped me to learn the communication of the wind and to realize my kinship with all beings. I am in your debt."

With tears in my eyes, I bowed my head to honor the wise bird and the gifts he had given me. He bowed to me as well to honor the help I had given him in nursing his wing back to health. Then he bowed to Humphrey, who immediately bowed back. "I hope you'll come back to visit me someday," I said to Ronnie. But Ronnie looked at me with his head cocked to one side and a glint in his eye, and without warning he let out an ear-piercing screech as he launched himself into the air, flapping his great wings and then soaring at high speed into a large arcing turn.

At the moment of Ronnie's screeching takeoff, two things happened to me at once. My awareness flew with the eagle so that I felt like I had jumped off the cliff with him, and Humphrey grabbed me by the shoulders from behind so that I wouldn't physically fall.

As I stood on the cliff with Humphrey supporting me, I had the most amazing experience of flying with Ronnie. I felt like I was inside the eagle's head, looking out at the world through his eyes. Somehow I could see what he was seeing as he soared in great spirals high above the land. I could feel the wind as we soared—my balance shifted as we made turns—and I could see with pinpoint accuracy everything that Ronnie was seeing below us.

Off in front and to the left, I saw far below us an interesting shimmer of light coming from an area near the town where I lived. As soon as I saw this, Ronnie immediately began to fly toward it. We were flying so high above the town that the cars and people were little more than specks below us. But I could identify buildings and houses very easily, except for a large area in town that seemed to be covered with a dome of shimmering light that I couldn't see into. I felt immediately drawn to the place, and as we flew in a few circles high above it, Ronnie let out a loud screech and then began to fly back in the direction of the cliff where we had released him.

We gradually flew toward the high mountain cliff, and as we got nearer, I could see myself and Humphrey standing on the ledge. But just then Ronnie dove down toward the base of the mountain, and I could see the tops of the trees growing closer as we descended.

Ronnie landed on the bare branch of a large, dead tree. We were facing the bottom of the cliff, and I could see a small, dark opening in the sheer rock face. As soon as I noticed it, I felt a sudden jolt of fright. But Ronnie was staring intently into the little cave, so I was forced to look with him. I noticed that all around the cave, in a wide area, it was darker than the rest of the land. It felt to me like all the energy and life of this place had been sucked up by the dark cave. I was just about to pass out from fright when Ronnie jumped from the tree and flew upwards again, toward the cliff that Humphrey and I were standing on. I didn't have time to try and explain to myself what had just happened because Ronnie flew right toward us and landed on my outstretched arm.

As soon as he landed on my arm, my awareness was back in my own body and I was looking at Ronnie sitting on my arm. Humphrey was still holding on to my shoulders for safety, and he whispered into my ear to keep my attention on Ronnie.

Just then, Ronnie again flew off of my arm and straight up into the air. This time, my awareness stayed with me as I watched Ronnie fly in five perfect circles high above my head. Then, in one sweeping motion, he darted straight down toward me and, with a loud screech, flew just over the top of my head and then straight up and away with the speed of an arrow. At that moment, I watched in sheer wonder as two beautiful feathers from Ronnie's wings dropped effortlessly into my hands. For a few seconds I looked at the large feathers in disbelief, and when I looked back up into the sky, Ronnie was gone.

I silently said goodbye to my friend and, with tears in my eyes, I turned to face Humphrey. He gently guided me to sit down, with my back propped against the rock for support. It was then that I suddenly realized I was drenched in sweat and my body was shaking. Humphrey put his jacket over me and instructed me to breathe deeply. "Close your eyes and feel your body breathing and your heart beating," Humphrey said to me calmly. "Your awareness left your body when you took that flight with Ronnie, and you must sit here and focus on your breathing until you feel whole again."

It took me nearly half an hour of consciously breathing and feeling my heart beating inside my chest before I felt like standing up, but eventually my senses came back to me, and Humphrey and I began to walk slowly back to the truck.

He handed me a bottle of water, and as I took it, my eyes met his and I knew instantly that he had seen everything that had happened to me. "The eagle has given you some powerful gifts in return for helping him back to health," Humphrey said as we continued walking down the narrow path through the forest.

"But how is it possible that I was able to fly with Ronnie?" I asked excitedly.

"Simple. When Ronnie took off, he hooked onto the subtle energy that you radiate, and part of that energy extended out with him. That caused your consciousness to expand and your view of reality to shift. The possibility of joining Ronnie in flight wasn't part of your reality until the moment when Ronnie hooked your energy and extended your consciousness out to join him. You could say that in that moment your consciousness jumped into an alternate reality. In that reality, it was completely possible for you to fly with Ronnie—not only that, you actually did it."

"And these feathers—what do I do with them now?" I asked, still holding them in disbelief.

"That's something you'll have to find out for yourself," replied Humphrey, grinning knowingly. "But you can be sure that they are a powerful gift to be used for seeing. Eagles like Ronnie that can see don't often give their own feathers as gifts. Until you discover how to use them, you should keep them safe, along with your mirror. The mirror and the feathers are your first two tools for seeing. As you continue to learn about them, the tools themselves will teach you how they are to be used. As a final gesture to you, I will make sure that you receive a special case to keep your new tools safe in."

"A final gesture?" I questioned. "What do you mean by that?"

"Our time together is almost over," Humphrey replied. "We may see each other again at times, just as you may see Ronnie again someday. But similar to how you have sent Ronnie on his journey, so must I do the same for you; my part in your training is complete. I have introduced you to the seer's world and instructed you in the seer's strategy, according to the ways of the wind. I have helped you to become aware of your energy body, and Amy and I have communicated to you how science and spirit are now integrating. Now you have to continue on your journey; you've already seen where you are to go next. Seeing that was the eagle's real gift to you."

I thought about all that I had seen and felt on my incredible flight with Ronnie as Humphrey continued, "The eagle's gift of seeing pointed out to you two special places in this part of the world. These are called power places because of the unique concentration of energy that each holds. The first power place that you saw was luminous and bursting with energy. The second power place was dark and drawing in energy. You felt drawn to the first place and repulsed by the second. Someday you will have to travel into that dark cave that leads to the underworld, because it is important for you to know how to use the energy of those dark places to balance the energy of the light. But you do not have the strength for that journey yet. Right now, your path leads to the place of light, the place that you felt drawn to during your flight with the eagle. Your next task is to find that place and discover why Ronnie helped you to see where it is."

———•———

Muvieri

The next day, I went to the tree house, but neither Humphrey nor Amy was there. I really wanted to talk to either one of them, so I hung around for a while and then decided to take a walk in the forest. I wandered around and ended up on the trail down to the creek—the same trail that Amy had led me up on my first day at the tree house. When I got to the bottom of the hill, I was delighted to find Amy sitting on the very bench where we had met that first day. She was sitting very quietly and smiled at me as I came over to sit down next to her.

"Well, I would say that I'm surprised to see you here, but nothing surprises me about seers anymore," I said to Amy honestly.

"You've come a long way since the day we first met, James, and you have a long way yet to go. Last night, Humphrey told me that you received the eagle's gift and that your time here at the tree house is over. Since I am your usher into the seer's world, it's my duty to help prepare you for your next journey."

"What do you mean, you are my usher?"

"The seer who discovers another at the beginning of their path is the usher of that person for life. Since the first day we ran into each other, our fate has been tied together. The spirits wanted me to find you that day on the ski slope so that I would help usher you into this world. There are two things remaining to do before you leave this place and continue your journey. Do you have your eagle feathers and your *nierika* with you?"

"I have the feathers, but what's a nierika? Is it the mirror on a stick that Matziwa gave me?"

"That's right. When a mirror like that is made by a shaman like Matziwa, we call it a nierika. In our line of seers, we use many words from the shamanic culture of the Huichol. In the Huichol language, a nierika is a sacred portal of vision and seeing."

"What do you mean, 'by our line of seers'?"

"We can be said to be of Humphrey's lineage, as he is passing his knowledge down to us. Humphrey was taught by holy people while living in India, Peru, and Mexico. Since he spent the most time in Mexico living with the Huichol and was trained there as a singing shaman, his students—such as you and I—naturally use the same names for things as he does.

"You have already learned a little bit about how to use the nierika; now, it is time that you start to learn about the *muvieri*—the magical feather wand of the seer. But remember this, because it's very important: the tools of seeing, such as the nierika and the muvieri, don't do anything on their own. Their magic is that they help us to focus our attention and heighten our awareness to the interconnection of all life so that the ripple of our mind flows outward into the great ocean of mind-matter-spirit."

Amy stood up and reached into a beautifully decorated cloth bag that had been sitting beside her on the bench. She pulled out a meticulously crafted rectangular case that was about twelve inches long, four inches wide, and four inches high. It was made of woven reed and had two almost identical parts: a bottom that fit perfectly inside the top.

"This case is the house where my helpers live," Amy said as she lifted off the top of the case. "And this is one of my muvieris."

Amy carefully lifted the muvieri out of the case, held it up to the sun for a few moments, and then handed it to me.

"This is my muvieri of wind energy. It is an extremely personal and sacred item to me. I'm allowing you to handle it because I'm your usher and because the wind around here knows you and you know it."

The muvieri was very simply but carefully made. It had two eagle feathers that were attached at the quills by some type of string, and the string was attached to a polished stick of a kind of wood I had never seen before. The way the feathers were tied to the stick enabled them to "fly" in the breeze or when the muvieri was moved around by hand. At the top end of the muvieri were small, downy feathers positioned upwards and attached to the stick.

As I was examining the muvieri and moving it around in order to make the feathers fly, Amy commented that one day I would make a muvieri from Ronnie's feathers, but today was not that day. Then she put all her stuff away, grabbed her bag, and told me to follow her down to the stream. We stopped at a flat and open area next to the stream, where the sun was shining brightly and the stream was singing strongly.

"Now that you have your nierika and the feathers for your muvieri, you are going to need a special place to keep them, along with the other tools that will come to you during your journey. Since I am your usher, I have made for you this special case to house your tools of seeing."

Amy pulled a brand-new case from her bag and held it in her open hands so that I could see it. It was identical to the one she had.

"When Humphrey told me last night that you had received the eagle's gift, we spent the whole night making this case for you. The woven pattern of the reeds represents the strong bond that has developed between you and us. The only thing left to do is consecrate the feathers, the nierika, and their new house, which we call a *takwatsi*, with a blessing and song of intent."

"I don't know what to say," I said to Amy as a profound feeling of gratitude for Humphrey, Amy, and this special place arose inside of me.

"There's nothing that you need to say," replied Amy. "When this blessing is over, your task is to jump into the unknown just like Ronnie did, and find your next task on your path, with heart."

While saying this, she carefully placed a beautiful piece of multicolored cloth on the ground, and then put my takwatsi on the cloth and removed its lid. She then instructed me to lay my nierika and my feathers inside the takwatsi so that she could bless them.

Amy took out her muvieri from its case and, while chant-singing a prayer of blessing to the wind, water, earth, and fire, she held up the muvieri to the sun while moving it in five large circles above her head. I stood in awe of the grace and power that Amy exuded as she carried out her movements, and I caught a glimpse of a shimmering light coming from the feathers of the muvieri as they flew in the air.

When she had completed the five circles in the air with the muvieri, she bent over and touched the tip of the muvieri to each of my things that had been placed on the cloth. Then she walked over to the stream and dipped the end of the muvieri in the water. She made five circles in the water and then touched the tip of the muvieri to my things once again. Amy also blessed my tools with five drops of deer blood for earth energy and five sprinkles of cedar ash for fire energy.

When she was finished with my tools, she did the same type of blessing for me, and then she quickly packed up her things and said goodbye. I was shaken by the finality of the moment and the thought of not seeing her again. I had come to truly appreciate, admire, and even love Amy and Humphrey. It was hard to imagine leaving them for my "new" task they kept talking about, but it seemed I had no choice.

*Of all that is written, I love only
what a person has written with
his own blood.*
FRIEDRICH NIETZSCHE

CHAPTER 2
Blood:
Medicine of Life and Death

Seeing, touching, smelling, and tasting blood are some of the most powerfully visceral experiences for living beings on our planet, so it's not to be wondered why it is simultaneously considered sacred and taboo for human beings. Such was the case with Nietzsche, who took much criticism for the above quote even though it was simply an allegory. But for most indigenous tribes and shamanic cultures throughout the world, the life-giving qualities of blood are ritually employed in ceremonies, divination, festivals, and blessings. In contrast, the world's three most dominant religions (Islam, Christianity, Judaism), in their strictest forms, forbid the consumption of blood as per the Qur'an, the Old Testament, and the Hebrew bible, although most Christians do not consider themselves to be bound by the Levitical purity code for various reasons.

As the fluid that transmits the necessary substances for life to the bodies of all mammals, birds, reptiles, and most fish on our planet, it carries the very basis of life no matter what spiritual tradition you acknowledge and therefore is the most tangible form of the numinous qualities of life that we could ever know.

Blood and Breath

Driving through the small town in rural Pennsylvania, I had the distinct impression I was being guided or even drawn to a special, sacred place. At the edge of town, suddenly, and without knowing why, I pulled over and parked in front of a large hedge of finely trimmed bushes that ran for at least a quarter of a mile along the side of a sidewalk that abruptly ended at the end of town. Following the high bushes, I walked down the sidewalk about twenty yards until I came to a driveway. More bushes and large trees blocked my view of where the driveway went, but on a white fence framing the driveway was a sign that read MARGARET LOUIS, N. MD, 166 NORTH MAIN STREET. I peered down the driveway and felt immediately attracted to the large trees and lush foliage ahead of me. The driveway curved to the right as I walked, and then suddenly in front of me appeared a picture-perfect old farmhouse. It was as though I had stepped through a secret doorway into a place unaffected by the outside world.

But by far the most amazing thing was that the whole area—the house, the barn, the outbuildings, the grounds, everything—radiated a barely perceptible luminous glow of shimmering light. All at once, I gasped at the thought that I had actually found the place that I had seen while flying with Ronnie. I stood in front of the main house, rubbing my eyes in disbelief at how such a beautiful and magical place could exist, especially so close to town. I gradually began to see that the brightest area of light seemed to be coming from an area behind the main house. My curiosity to see where the light was coming from was so great that I immediately headed for the back of the house. There was a cobblestone path leading in that direction, so I followed it until I was stopped in my tracks by the most beautiful garden and orchard I had ever seen. I stood there, looking in amazement at the orchard in full bloom and the garden gleaming in the sunlight, when I noticed that about twenty yards away there was a woman kneeling on the ground, working in one of the rows of flowering plants.

Maggie, aside from being a licensed naturopathic physician with many clients, was a wizened old medicine woman of Seneca blood. She owned the large orchard and many small organic gardens on her property, and during certain times of the year she would take on apprentices to learn about gardening and working the land and such.

"When I woke up this morning," Maggie began while shaking my hand firmly, "I just knew it was going to be a special day, with you finding your way here. Seers that come to this area are eventually drawn here by the special energy of this place, and you are no exception—except for the fact that you are still in your first stages of learning. Therefore, you being here carries much significance for us both."

As if walking in a dream, Maggie and I strolled the grounds and talked for what had to have been hours. I felt a sense of comfort with her that I had rarely experienced before, and to this day I still don't remember all that we talked about during our first meeting. Being in that special place where everything was literally bursting with life and energy, coupled with the magical presence and air of powerful femininity exuded by Maggie, had certainly placed me in an altered state of consciousness.

"There's lots of work to do around here, James," Maggie said as our tour of the property was ending. "The plants in the garden need care, the orchard needs to be pruned, and there's a continual need for making the plant medicines I use for my clients. Would you like to work for me for a while?

"Before you accept my invitation," Maggie continued, "you must realize that the job I'm offering you is not only to earn money. It is also the next step in your training to become a seer. You have learned a lot very quickly, but I believe that with sufficient intent and guidance, this land will teach you many more things, and you will come from this experience much more grounded and with a greater sense of your place in the world, which is what you are needing in your life right now. Are you ready to accept the job as well as the challenges?"

I was so fascinated by Maggie, and her property was so special, that I didn't even think twice about saying yes, even though I had no idea what I was really getting myself into.

I told Maggie I was ready, and the next day at 6 AM I arrived at her place. I was in total shock to find Amy sitting with Maggie on a bench outside of the laboratory building where she made her natural remedies and potions. I had no idea that Amy even knew Maggie.

"Good morning, Jim," they both said as I walked up.

I returned their greeting and must have had a puzzled look on my face because they both chuckled slightly at me.

"Amy is one of my students," Maggie explained. "And since she's also your usher into the seer's world, it's important that she be here and with you during certain moments of your training." Astounded as I was at this turn of events, I had little choice but to simply go with the flow.

Maggie wasn't kidding when she said there was a lot of work to do in the gardens and the orchard. Every morning I would arrive at the main house and she would have a list of things for me to do that day. There was watering, pruning, lawn cutting, composting, fertilizing, maintaining equipment, repairing tools, and picking up supplies, to name a few. Some days I would work with Maggie or Amy, sometimes with both, and sometimes with other students that would come and go, but Maggie made sure that each day I spent at least a few hours alone working with the plants and trees of the land.

One morning after I had been working there for about a month, Maggie pulled me aside and said, "The plants and trees here are getting to know you, Jim, so from now on, it's especially important for you to pay attention for any signs that they may give you. A plant spirit may make a gesture toward you. This gesture could feel as slight as being brushed by a feather or as direct as being hit with a bat; it all depends on which spirit is talking to you. But it's up to you to hear with your heart what the spirit is trying to tell you."

Later that day, I was working with Amy and she was showing me how to prune the rose bushes that grew along the fence in the southern end of the herb garden. On the very first bush I began to prune, I cut my finger on one of its thorny branches.

"Be careful!" Amy exclaimed as she looked over and saw me put my finger in my mouth to stop the bleeding. "You've got to pay close attention when you're pruning these bushes. It's not like pruning a pear tree. These thorns are sharp!"

The cut was small and the bleeding stopped quickly. But when I was finished with the first bush and began the second one, I immediately cut myself again on the same hand.

"Maybe I should wear some gloves," I said to Amy as she worked expertly on another bush.

"That's cheating," she replied with a grin. "Besides, you're supposed to be learning about plants, and the best way to start doing that is to be in physical contact with them. You'll get the hang of it. Just be more careful."

I cut myself again when starting on the third bush and also the fourth. When I got to the fifth bush, I just knew that no matter how hard I concentrated I was still going to get cut by the bush as soon as I started. I was standing there, looking at it fearfully, when Maggie walked up.

"How are you making out?" she asked cheerfully.

"You mean *besides* being cut by every bush I've pruned so far?" I replied sarcastically.

"Maybe the bushes want something from you," Maggie said cryptically.

We looked at each other, and she smiled. I waited for an explanation, but she remained silent. Finally I had to tell her that I didn't understand.

"Maybe the bushes are asking for your blood," Maggie said with a raise of her eyebrows and a comical expression on her face.

"What could the rose bushes possibly want with my blood?" I asked in surprise.

"Blood carries the life force," replied Maggie, "and it is also a potent symbol. If the plant spirit of the roses wants to get to know you, there is nothing that carries your energy more personally than your own blood. If you were to give a few drops of your blood to the soil of the plants, your energy would mix with theirs and they would grow with some of your energy inside of them. If the rose plants are really asking this of you, it is an extremely special sign that they wish to be your ally. There's really only one way to find out if that's what they have in mind."

Maggie quickly snipped a small section of thorny branch from the bush that was next for me to prune and handed it to me. She told me to prick my finger and let five drops of blood fall into the soil at the base of the plant. I followed her instructions and then she told me to go ahead and try pruning the bush. I pruned the whole bush and didn't get cut once. Then I pruned another and didn't get cut by that one either.

"Well, I think that answers that question," Maggie said triumphantly. "It seems you've found your first plant spirit ally. This is truly wonderful," she added happily. "Now give a drop to the other four plants that asked you for some, but this time use your breath as well while you are doing it. Blood is activated by breath, and so they always go together. It's a very powerful combination."

"How do I use my breath, Maggie?" I asked.

"By talking or singing with your heart through your voice," answered Maggie. "Just use your voice while you offer them a few drops of your blood. There is no way to use your voice without exhaling. If you are talking or singing, then you are automatically breathing. In fact, if I read the signs of this situation correctly, these rose bushes are going to teach you some important things, and you would be wise to spend some time each day using your voice with them and also listening to them with your heart."

Amy and I trimmed more than twenty bushes while I gave them my breath, and I didn't cut myself once.

The roses flowered a few weeks later, and Maggie taught me how to make rose beads and a necklace with them. She told me that the rose beads had the magical gift of the blood connection I shared with the soil and the spirits of the plants. If I wore them or carried them with me, I would always be reminded of the interconnection of all life, and thus my decisions and actions would reflect that knowledge and the sacred connection of blood and breath.

———————◆———————

Old John Redcorn

Old John Redcorn was of the Lenni Lenape tribe of Oklahoma. But when I first met John, he was living in Pennsylvania, as he had wanted to live for a spell in the woods where his ancestors once lived. The story of the gracious Lenape (also known as the Delaware) people is a sad one. They were some of the first "Indians" to help the haggard seamen from Europe that arrived to the "New World" to survive in the 1600s, but their kindness has never been returned. Decade after decade and centuries later, they were slowly but surely pushed off their ancestral lands by the White Man, and now scarcely a few even remember their ancient traditions or lifestyles. John Redcorn was one of the few who did.

One day in my early twenties, I saw an advertisement for a local event about Indian culture at a state park near the Delaware River. I lived close to the park and knew it well. The event turned out to be quite interesting, with mini courses on Lenape canoe making, flintknapping, basket weaving, etc.

As I flipped through the pamphlet of programs, I saw there was a fire-making course starting in a few minutes, so I headed over to that area, and that's where I first met Old John Redcorn. He was the first person to ever really teach me how to make fire without matches. John's preferred method was the bow drill, at which he was a master.

As a Boy Scout, I had learned about making fire, but the techniques had never really stuck with me, and if I was lost in the woods, I doubt if I could have made a fire without matches or a lighter. John Redcorn remedied that. The old man was so passionate and so good at teaching that I have never forgotten what he taught me, and I have actually taught many others over the years what John shared with me about making a fire.

Remarkably, after that first meeting, John and I kept in touch, though not very often. Looking back, John had an uncanny way of writing me a letter just before I was about to move somewhere. It was because of this, some fifteen years later, that my girlfriend Sue and I were on our way to his house in Missouri while visiting Arizona from the East Coast.

As we pulled into the driveway, John must have been waiting because he came dashing out, motioning for us to be quiet and to follow him. It was a dark but clear night, and John led us to the back of his rural house, seemingly situated in a large hay field. But as my eyes adjusted to the dark, I began to see that there were many fruit trees and also a large garden (yes, probably with some red corn) off to the left of the house.

After only a minute or so, it became apparent what John wanted to show us. His nephew Tim—who looked just like him, only twenty years younger—was out back as well, and he joined us as we all watched four coyotes and a single badger toying with a squirrel that was badly injured by the gang of carnivores but was still alive. For whatever reason, right then neither the coyotes nor the badger seemed in a hurry for a meal of squirrel; they preferred to just play with the unfortunate squirrel, tossing it into the air, picking it up lightly, and shaking and pawing at it.

This was the first and only time I ever saw a badger "playing." I had seen coyotes do all kinds of strange and funny things before, but never a badger, as they are typically ornery, antisocial creatures known to be so fierce that they can fight off wolves and even bears. I looked intently at John Redcorn, and he whispered to us with a snicker, "That badger is drunk from all the rotten fruit he ate earlier." And the more I watched the badger, it seemed that John was right—the badger *was* kind of stumbling around and seeming to lack coordination.

Well, the poor squirrel finally died, and the coyotes made a quick meal of him. The badger didn't seem to mind that they didn't share it with him. He just turned and started to amble away. Just then, one of the larger coyotes perked up, and I could swear I saw a mischievous—or even malicious—

gleam in his eye. From the look of it, the taste of blood had gotten him riled up, and the squirrel was nothing more than a snack. He was licking his lips and paws while eyeing the badger as he walked away.

But Mr. Coyote was not going to let him go. He snuck up on the badger and bit him square on the backside. The badger turned fiercely and puffed himself up, teeth unfurled. He was more than a formidable opponent even for four coyotes, and they all knew it. However, the lead coyote must have sensed that there was something a bit off about this badger tonight, just like John had said, because it proceeded to rally its friends, and after a fierce but fairly quick fight, the coyotes killed the badger, ripped open his belly, and began to feed on him.

Old John Redcorn said he wanted the badger pelt, so he grabbed a garden shovel and scared off the coyotes. The rest of us walked over to the slain badger, where John was kneeling over it and saying some prayers in a language I didn't understand. The moon was about half full that night, and with the sky being clear it was bright enough that I could easily see the quizzical look on John's face as he stood up, and I knew then that the death of the badger wasn't the only thing we were going to see that night.

There was a large pool of blood on the hard, dry earth next to the badger's open guts. John Redcorn began to explain to us that in ancient times his people would look into the blood of a badger and sometimes see the future. He invited us to try it if we wanted, and he said he'd go first. John positioned himself so he could see his reflection off the light of the moon in the blood. From where I was standing, I could see his reflection as well. I didn't see the future or anything else, and apparently neither did he. All I saw was John's reflection. But as he stood up, I caught that quizzical look of his again, and I wondered if he had seen more than I did…

Next went John Jr. He knelt over the blood, and what I saw was astounding: the reflection of John Jr. was him—but as an old man! He must have seen the same thing as he gasped and moved away from the blood. Old John Redcorn had a huge grin on his face.

I went next, but for some odd reason a cloud suddenly obscured the moon, and I could see nothing in the blood. I asked John if we could wait for the cloud to pass, but he said no, that we had seen what we were supposed to see tonight about life and death.

Old John Redcorn was right, and the blood had showed it. Old John died not six months later, looking exactly as he did in his reflection that night. And his nephew John is still alive and kicking at close to seventy years old, and he looks exactly like his reflection we saw in the badger's blood on that magical night.

———◆———

Healing by Quwi

Historians tell us that the cute little guinea pig, now a common pet in Western societies, was originally domesticated sometime around 5000 BC in the Andean region of South America that is present-day Ecuador, Peru, and Bolivia. It is debatable how the guinea pig got its English name, for it is neither a pig nor from Guinea. It's actually classified scientifically as a rodent belonging to the family Caviidae.

For many thousands of years, this furry, diminutive creature has been employed as food, revered as a sacred animal, and used in healing ceremonies and rituals. Its stature as an important part of Andean society still lives on today in the same capacities. Although "modern" people may see the culinary and ritual use of the guinea pig as taboo, its high protein and low fat content, as well as the relative ease of raising them, has made them a valued market commodity in the Andes and throughout the world. It is conservatively estimated that there are over 30 million guinea pigs being raised just in the country of Peru!

In most parts of the rural Andes, healthcare as we know it is basically nonexistent or culturally rejected. If a sick individual can't be cured by household remedies, the patient is almost always taken to a shaman–folk healer known as a curandero (male) or curandera (female). The practice of *curanderismo* is found almost everywhere in Latin America, and the spectrum of healing practices includes herbs and natural medicines, divination, entheogens, animal sacrifice, oils, incense, and, most importantly, the healer's ability to work with the "supernatural." In curanderismo, ill health is attributed to disequilibrium or disharmony within the person or their relationship with outside forces. In the Andes, one of the most favored and popular forms of diagnosis and treatment is the folk doctor's use of the guinea pig, or *quwi* in the native language.

This is the story of my first healing by an Andean curandera using the medium of a quwi in both diagnosis and treatment. At the time I was not seriously ill, but I had a few nagging problems and sought medical attention. In this remote location of the Peruvian Andes, the only choice was the local folk doctor, and I was brought by my friends to see her. Arriving at her house, I had a sore throat, phlegm in my chest, and my left leg was very stiff and sore and both of my feet were extremely dry, cracked, calloused, and sore from weeks of walking in the mountains. It was a Tuesday morning, one of two days a week the curandera did this type of healing, and there were at least twenty people in line to see her. My Peruvian friends talked to the people in line and explained to them I was only in the area for a short time, and very graciously the people let me—even encouraged me—to the front of the line. Leaving my friends at the door and walking into the healer's room felt like stepping into a different world of time and space. Paradoxically, my memory of the healing is etched deeply into my mind and at the same time seems like a vague recollection. Here's what I remember:

The curandera Doña Antonia had a table placed in the corner of the room where all of her healing paraphernalia had been placed. Next to the table, a young woman sat in a chair with a cloth in her lap with what appeared to be plant leaves on top of it. The only light in the room was from many candles placed in various locations. I had no idea what the younger woman was doing there. Doña Antonia noticed my glances at the woman and explained that the woman was training to be a curandera, so during the healing sessions that day, the apprentice would sit in silence and observe while chewing on coca leaves in order to reinforce the power of healing through the quwi.

A beautiful handwoven blanket was spread out on the floor, and Doña Antonia instructed me to take off my shirt and lie down on the blanket.

Then she took a bunch of fresh flowers from her table and passed them all over my body to ward off evil spirits and make me calm and receptive. Next came the quwi (also known as *jaca* or *cuy* in Spanish). I was instructed to roll over, face down, and the most exceptional feeling commenced as Doña Antonia rubbed the live, soft, furry quwi up and down my body from head to toe many times. When it touched the skin of my bare back, neck, and feet, I could feel that it was alive, but in my mind's eye I didn't see or imagine a quwi in Doña Antonia's hands—I'm not sure what I felt except that it felt pure and full of energy. I had not yet seen the quwi Doña Antonia was using on me.

Next, she instructed me to roll onto my back, and I saw that she was using a black quwi, one of the rarest colors, but to some curanderas the most useful, especially for adults or for those that have never been healed by a quwi before. Doña Antonia rubs the black quwi all over my face, chest, arms, and legs for about ten minutes and then sits me up. Sometimes during this part of the ritual, the rubbing of the quwi (*jaca shoqpi*), the quwi will actually die. But in this case the quwi is still alive, and Doña Antonia declares that to be a good sign.

Doña Antonia took the quwi to her *mesa* (table) and, standing it upright, she slit its throat while offering prayers of thanks to the quwi's spirit and collecting its blood in a small cup as she turned it upside down. Then she skinned the quwi from the neck down so perfectly that the hide was completely intact and still connected at the quwi's feet. She then took the quwi, skin and all, and rinsed it in a basin of clean water. Even though it was now dead, the quwi seemed to tremble slightly, and a thin, milky white membrane formed on its back as I watched. Doña Antonia seemed pleased by this and told me that it was a sign that my cold had passed from me and into the quwi. But she wanted to examine more, so she slit open the quwi and inspected the organs.

Other than the cold that had been removed from my body by the quwi, the diagnosis of stiff joints in my left leg and dry, cracked feet and the treatments needed were made through an analysis of the quwi's organs. Doña Antonia once again took her knife and cut a small portion of fat from the quwi and handed it to her apprentice, who placed it into a large metal spoon and heated it by placing the spoon over a finely decorated candle. When the fat was more or less liquefied, Doña Antonia had me sit in a chair, and she dipped her fingers into the fat and spread it into the cracks of my feet, paying special attention to the large cracks on my heals.

With that done, she treated my stiff joints by mixing the blood of the quwi with some sweet wine. Doña Antonia told me that I suffered from a mild case of arthritis and that the quwi-wine mixture would help; she told me to drink the whole cup, which I did.

Finally, she stood me up and sprayed my entire body with a fragrant water by taking a large quantity of the water into her mouth and then spit-spraying me with it multiple times. I had experienced this type of spraying with other healers using an alcohol-based mixture, so I wasn't surprised by it, but each experience is unique, and the flower-water mixture of Doña Antonia felt and smelled really good.

Doña Antonia announced that my healing was a success but would continue only if I followed some simple rules for three days: not shaking hands with anyone and no bathing. The no-bathing part would not be difficult, as I often went three days or more while in the Andes without showering or bathing, but the thought of not shaking anyone's hands for three days seemed almost impossible with all the traveling I had planned and all the new people I would be meeting. I had visions of people thinking of me as a rude American who refused to shake their hands; I wouldn't get very far if people perceived me that way. However, Doña Antonia saw the look on my face and casually told me that everyone I would meet in the mountains would understand. For example, for some people of importance—such as government officials who didn't want to openly declare their trust in the curandera's folk remedies—it was common to say that one had hurt or fractured their right wrist and therefore couldn't shake. To make me more comfortable about the whole thing, Doña Antonia wrapped my wrist with a piece of cloth in the same way she would have if I actually had a fractured wrist, and I felt much better.

"People are going to know anyway what you are up to, but it won't matter either way, and in some cases if they know you are open to our traditional ways, it might even help you," Doña Antonia said in a soothing voice.

"But what about my left hand?" I blurted out at the thought.

"That's easy," she replied, chuckling. "Keep it in your pocket."

And with that, I said thanks to Doña Antonia and her apprentice, gave her the appropriate fee for her services, and left. Once outside and when my Andean friends had finished laughing at what they knew was my fake wrist bandage, I distinctly noticed how much better I felt. The congestion had loosened remarkably in my chest, my throat no longer hurt, I felt I had more energy than I'd had in many days, my sore leg felt fine, and my feet still hurt some as I walked but not nearly as much as before. All in all, Doña Antonia made me a believer in the power of the simple little creature called quwi and in her skill at administering this ancient folk-healing practice. Now I fully comprehended why people wait in line for several hours every Tuesday and Friday to see her and be healed by her magical quwi.

Please note: The disposal of a quwi that has died during a healing ceremony is always treated in a sacred way. Much of what happens to the body is a secret known only to the curandera, but what I do know is that it is customary for the curandera to replace the skin of the quwi exactly how it was when alive, wrap up the quwi and the same flowers used in the healing in paper or cloth, and then take it far from the village and into the wilderness. While no one is watching, the curandera returns the body of the quwi and the *tikrapay* (the illness absorbed by the quwi) to Mother Nature.

A true initiation never ends...
ROBERT ANTON WILSON

CHAPTER 3
Initiation:
Medicine of Transformation

Sometimes hilarious, sometimes deadly, but always enlightening, initiations in their various forms are an indispensable part of shamanic medicine teachings. Initiations can be very formal occasions, such as rites of passage that an initiate long prepares for and the whole community knows about and supports. On the other hand, initiations can be extremely personal and/or spontaneous. In the following stories, I have included some samples of both, but in all cases, the results of the initiations transformed my life forever.

Cosmic Clowns

I invited a revered holy man from the Arapaho tribe to stay with me in Sedona for a few weeks and do some talks and healings in order to make some money to care for his grandmother, who had cancer and could not afford traditional medical treatment (which, by the way, she didn't want anyway). But there were still items and food necessary for her upcoming passing ceremony, so I gladly invited Highwater to come and share his dances, rituals, and stories for the exchange of energy (money) that people would pay to see him.

I had met Highwater when I was a young buck living as a ski bum near Winter Park, Colorado. At the time, I was sharing a small hotel room in a little rickety joint in Fraser with a friend, and since I didn't have a car, I hitchhiked every morning to the ski resort some fifteen miles away. Fraser is one of the coldest places in the wintertime in the United States, and one morning I was standing outside the hotel, freezing my ass off, with my thumb out, when he picked me up in his dilapidated pickup truck on the little two-lane road in the middle of nowhere.

I had no idea who he was at the time, and in that moment I really didn't care; I was just thankful for the ride. But our connection was immediate. He showed me kindness and respect and gave me some warm coffee from his Thermos.

Highwater was an extraordinary man. Later, through the years, he shared with me many ancient and sacred items of his people that few "whites" had ever seen. Every time he picked me up hitchhiking, it was like a ceremony, and one way or another he would get some bit of wisdom in during our conversation that I would use during the course of my day.

I was delighted that years later he was coming to my home and that I could return some of the favors he had given to me in the past. However, I also knew that with Highwater it was not going to be a picnic; he was quick to laugh and joke around, but his methods of teaching were equally powerful. I knew in my gut that something big would happen when he visited.

The night he arrived, it was very late, and we shared a couple sips of whiskey on my couch in front of the fire of my woodstove. Then he unrolled his blanket, curled up on the couch, and said good night. But just as I turned away, he sat up and, with an intense look, said, "Sweet dreams."

I didn't think much of that comment but went to bed and fell quickly asleep. That night I had lucid dreams of thunder and lightning and a giant horse that ran right at me and struck me down, then turned around and ran back, trampling me to death.

I woke up in the middle of the night in a cold sweat and walked out to the kitchen to get some water. I was so focused on drinking water that I didn't notice Highwater as I walked through the living room. But after I chugged two glasses of water and turned to go back to bed, I saw Highwater sitting up on the couch, staring into the fire.

"Come here and sit, boy," he said in a faraway voice.

I sat next to the holy man, and he asked me what I had just dreamed. I explained what I had seen, and he let out a big sigh. He put his face in his hands and bent over as if feeling terribly sad. But for some reason I felt like he was simply pretending to be sad and that he was actually grinning inside.

"You have dreamt of the opposite ones. This is powerful medicine that cannot be ignored. It is one of the most difficult tests in the life of a young medicine man. Now you have to live the life of a contrary. Everything you do must be the opposite of everything you know. This seems silly to 'civilized' people, but it is one of the most sacred acts to us Arapaho. The Hopi also do it in their *kachina* dances where the clown, the opposite, makes fun of everything. But in his fun-making, he is one of the most sacred dancers. To our relatives the Dakota, when someone has a dream like yours, they become *heyoka*, a thunder being that completely reverses typical behavior, for that is how one sees the second world, the world that others are blind to. In our Arapaho tradition, outsiders see the heyoka as a clown, a mere joke, but the sacred fool embodies the paradox of life and to us is seen as sacred. There is nothing more difficult than to be your opposite, and any man that can do it will eventually see the world with new eyes and embrace the cosmic paradox. This is what you will begin to do right now.

"You want to sit here by the fire with me, but now you need to go naked and sit outside in the dark and cold. Take off all your clothes and *go now!*"

I was totally bewildered by Highwater's words. I didn't want to go out into the cold, dark night, especially naked, but I did it anyway. I stripped down and lay on the couch on my front porch. There was already a blanket there, so I was relieved for that, and I brought my best friend—Sophie, my German shepherd—out with me, and we both curled up.

Not five minutes later, Highwater came out onto the porch, confiscated my blanket, and took Sophie inside with him.

"You are heyoka now," he said sternly. "You get no warmth, no comfort from your dog, and *no* sleep."

He handed me a piece of manzanita wood, also known as iron wood because it is so hard, and a small pocket knife.

"Whittle on this wood until the sun comes up, and if I catch you sleeping, I swear to god I will put you over my knee and spank you!"

I had no doubt in my mind that Highwater would do exactly what he promised, so I whittled that branch to nothing while shivering so hard in the cold that when the dawn came, I was never so happy in my life.

When he finally came out the front door onto the porch, to my great relief Highwater had a kind look on his face and was carrying my coffee mug. I couldn't wait to put my cold hands on it and drink the warm brew, but instead of handing me a nice hot cup of coffee, he threw an ice-cold cup of water in my face.

"Hahahaha! You are heyoka now, you little pissant! Now get in your truck and wait for me—we're going for a ride."

"But I have no clothes on!"

"That's right … and that's why it's going to be so incredibly fun!"

I was livid. But I walked to my truck naked, started it, and turned the heater on full blast as I sat in the driver's seat, barely able to keep my eyes open.

Highwater entered the truck soon after, slapped me hard in the face as he could see I was falling asleep, and immediately turned off the truck heater and put down all the windows. He was dressed in my warmest goosedown coat that he must have gotten from my closet, warm boots, and even gloves and a hat. Of course, I was still completely naked.

He then had me drive into town to buy gas. When we arrived at the station, he said he would go inside and pay so I wouldn't get arrested, but that I was to pump the gas.

"You really expect me to get out of this truck and pump gas in front of all these people?" I asked in fear.

"You are heyoka now. You have no fear. Once you completely embrace the opposite, then other people won't even be able to see your naked white penis flapping in the breeze."

I actually heard him laughing as he walked into the store and paid for the gas. Ironically, not one person even noticed there was a naked guy at the gas station filling up his truck.

So we headed down the road, and he told me to go to one of the most popular hiking trails in Sedona, where I could be recognized in a heartbeat by a number of people.

At this point, I am completely out of my mind, but Highwater was so strong and intimidating in the casual way that he does the most bizarre things that I was beyond even beginning to argue with him.

We arrived at the parking lot of the trailhead, and there were at least twenty cars there. "Get out and walk the trail," Highwater calmly said.

I got out of the truck, covering my genitals with my hands, and could hear Highwater walking behind me.

"Hey, heyoka!" he yelled to me. "You walk backwards. You do everything the opposite—you think opposite; you shit outside; and when you walk, you walk backwards!"

In that moment, I couldn't believe I had asked Highwater to come stay with me. I suddenly felt like he was a crazy person. But I did what he said and began walking the trail backwards. Even though there were so many cars in the parking lot, I walked backwards all the way around Cathedral Rock for about three hours and somehow did not encounter one person—or maybe I did and in my completely altered state didn't even see them, or maybe they couldn't see me. Most of the time while walking I felt like I was floating. The extreme circumstances of the situation had totally altered my consciousness.

Near the end of the backwards hike, we came to Oak Creek, and I was really thirsty. I stopped and bent down to drink. "Hey, heyoka!" Highwater yelled. "You are the opposite—first you spit and *then* you drink!"

We finally made it back to the truck, and he told me to drive home because I had previously arranged a speaking engagement for him, and he needed to get ready. I was surprised when he didn't tell me to drive home backwards…

"Go put on your best suit and tie," he instructed me when we got home.

"I only own one suit and tie," I replied.

"Well, go put it on, heyoka!"

"I can't go out in public to this event in a suit and tie! The only reason I even own it was for my sister's wedding years ago. I'm not even sure where it is!"

"Well, you better go find it, because that's what you're wearing tonight."

At the kind of event we were going to, *no one* would be in a suit and tie. They would all have on casual clothing and beaded Indian jewelry and turquoise and crystals; of course, Highwater knew that.

When we arrived at the event, Highwater was in full Arapaho regalia and the place was packed and ready for him. I, on the other hand, was in a wedding suit, feeling like a total idiot as we walked in. The owners of the bookstore where Highwater was going to speak are good friends of mine. When we walked in together, looking the way we did, they busted out laughing, and everyone else who knew me, seated in their chairs, waiting, busted out laughing too.

There was only one chair seated in front of the audience for Highwater to sit in if he wanted to, though I knew he wouldn't sit while he talked to the crowd. So he motioned for me to sit in it.

As I looked into the crowd and saw so many people I knew, and knowing how ridiculous it must have seemed to them to see me dressed that way and for Highwater to place me on the stage dressed like that, I finally got it. Highwater was a master at breaking down the proud side of a person's ego.

There is nothing to be ashamed of at being proud of something you do— an exquisite piece of art, a good book, a good deed, a simple kind word. But Highwater knew that the ego is a tricky animal, and my dream was interpreted by him as me needing to be broken down—to become more humble. To not be ashamed of being naked or looking like the fool.

Later, when we got home that night—and by the way, he did not let me talk on the drive home, because he knew that's exactly what I wanted to do—he made me sleep in my suit, and in the morning he shook me awake.

For the next week, he made me do and say everything the opposite. I could sleep in the day but not the night. When he asked me a question, I had to say no when I wanted to say yes. I had to shit outside where there was an anthill so they would crawl on me while I did my business. Cold showers. No phone calls. No computer. No visitors. Daily walks through town walking backwards (but not naked anymore).

Then he took me up to a small village on reservation land and put this mask on my face that looked like a seagull on acid, and he paraded me around the village while telling me to flap my arms like a bird. (In actuality, the mask was a caricature of the Thunderbird, a sacred and symbolic being closely associated with heyoka ritual in many native cultures.)

I could see out of the small eyeholes of this ridiculous-looking mask, so I could see and hear all the people laughing at me. But truth be told, I didn't care anymore. The ridicule was sacred. These people knew what Highwater was doing to me. They laughed anyway because it was still damn funny to see this white guy in a silly bird mask dancing around, flapping his wings, with an old Indian holy man kicking him in the butt the whole time.

After parading me around the whole village, with most of the village people now following us, Highwater instructed the children that were following us to go get buckets of water, and they created a giant mud hole in the middle of the village.

Then they all surrounded me, and I had flashbacks of being in a large mosh pit at a rock concert. And to my dismay, my flashback soon turned into a strange reality as the biggest warriors of the tribe joined in and began throwing me into the mud. Every time I would stagger up, they threw me in again until I was a totally muddy mess.

Then, to my utter surprise, most of the young warriors stripped off all of their clothes, the children stripped me of mine, and for the next half-hour or so, we had a crazy brawl naked in the mud.

All ego was left behind. Naked men playing in the mud, tackling each other, throwing mud at each other, with no maliciousness, just pure unadulterated fun of the kind rarely experienced by "civilized" people.

Afterwards, Highwater took a hose and hosed us all clean.

The men all patted me on the back and said, "You have learned to be heyoka, a cosmic clown without inhibitions, just like us. Next time someone comes to be heyoka, you are welcome to come and dance the mud bath with us."

<hr />

Fire Hawk

I first met Fire Hawk, a Minnecojou Sioux, when I was somewhere around sixteen years old, traveling across the country with two friends, mostly walking and hitchhiking. Sometimes a kind person would lend us a car for a few days. A couple times, we stole a car for a few days and then called the police to tell them where they could find it. My friends and I were reckless, and we liked to drink sometimes, so we would get into fights if someone got in our faces, but we really didn't want to hurt anyone so we were basically nice to people and always gave the car back if we stole one. But mostly we just walked and camped along the way.

One day, we found ourselves on the outskirts of the Badlands in South Dakota. Even though we were under the legal drinking age, the three of us walked into a rickety old shack that had the word "bar" painted on a crude sign over the door. No one there paid special attention to us. There were only a few older guys in there, who all looked to be of Indian blood, and since we had money, the big, surly barkeep served us some beers without question.

But then things took a turn as a bunch of young Natives walked into the bar, got their beers, and began to leer at us. The smallest but toughest-looking one came over to our table as the others surrounded us, and in the most impolite fashion, he informed us we were not welcome in their bar or on their land and to get the hell out.

Well, my friend Todd, who was the toughest of our small group, was not used to backing down to anyone and invited him, in an equally impolite fashion, to step outside and resolve the matter man-to-man. Todd stood up and threw his chair back, but to our dismay all the Native guys drew their knives that had been hidden in the back of their pants. We were unarmed, and I began to have a really bad feeling about the whole situation. I was not afraid to fight—in fact, back then I actually kind of liked it, because I was a good fighter and rarely ever lost. But this scene had the makings to turn really ugly, so I calmly got up from my chair and walked over to the barkeep and told him in a quiet voice to please offer the boys a beer on us, in their own language, as a peace offering, because we were not there to intrude or to fight.

The barkeep summed up the situation real fast. Here were three white guys who were not going to back down. He could tell we were not some sissy college boys out for a joy ride. We would give as good as we got, and if it came to fighting, there would be blood shed for sure. So he complied with my request, but the Natives didn't back off one bit.

Luckily for everyone, an old man sitting at the end of the bar came over and whispered "Nice try" in my ear, and then, with a slight motion of his head, he signaled the Native boys to back off. I still remember the look of the tough guy who originally picked the fight as the old man signaled him to stop—he looked like he was going to piss his pants when he saw the old guy giving him the silent order. He was still mad, but he and all his friends retreated and went to the bar to get their free beers.

I went back to our table, and the old man followed me. I offered him a beer, but he waved it off. That was the day I met Fire Hawk. The old man just sat there, staring at me drinking my beer, until finally I had enough of his scrutiny.

"Thanks for your help back there, old man, but really—what is your problem? I don't like people staring at me."

"We have been fighting for too long, your people and mine. I am trying to figure out what is different about you that I am feeling right now. Come, step outside with me for a minute."

Of course, in that moment I felt much trepidation at his request. It could have been some sort of trap. But looking at the old man and the way the young, rowdy Natives obviously were respectful and even fearful of him, I decided to take him up on his offer. I told my friends to just sit tight and be cool, and I walked outside with the old man.

There were a few chairs outside, and he asked me to pull two of them up so we could sit down. Then he began to ask me a series of questions that gave me the distinct impression that he was a trained psychologist or psychotherapist, even though he I suspected he had no college degree. I learned later that in terms of academic studies, his education was at about a sixth-grade level. But little did I know at the time that he had a lifetime of experience as a medicine man, and he drew out of me that I was a first-generation American born of parents who were both from Hungary, that my father had tragically died a few years back, and a whole lot of other things that seemed pointless to me at the time. The only thing I learned from him was that he was a medicine man. That's all he would say when I asked him something: "I am a medicine man just doing my job."

Many years after I first met Fire Hawk, I did something really stupid. For almost a year after moving into a new house, I had problems with my next-door neighbor. Without going into details, suffice it to say we did not like each other and did not get along. One day, we finally got in a physical altercation, and in the aftermath, my neighbor's wife called the police.

While two officers questioned me, two others questioned him and his wife. Then all the officers huddled together, and after a few minutes, to my utter astonishment, they handcuffed me and threw me in the back of a police car. I couldn't believe it and asked for an explanation, because my neighbor had come onto my property, and he had begun the fight. But the police didn't care. They only saw that I didn't have a scratch on me and that his face was a bloody mess, even though he was about six foot three and 300 pounds and I was 165 pounds soaking wet.

I was charged with disorderly conduct and spent the night in jail. It was totally humiliating. Since there were no witnesses to the actual fight or who had started it, I had no choice but to plead guilty to the charge and pay a large fine in order not to remain in jail.

Needless to say, I was devastated. After spending the whole night in jail thinking about what had just happened, I was furious—but mostly I was just disappointed in myself. I should have just walked away instead of fighting. I was an adult now and becoming a well-known healer and guide. When I got home, I was feeling very depressed and drained, and I slumped down onto my couch.

A few minutes later, the phone rang, and it was Fire Hawk calling! After we shared a few pleasantries, he told me in a calm but concerned voice that he had a dream the night before about me. In the dream, he saw me as a caged animal pacing back and forth in captivity, and he was worried about me.

Of course, I proceeded to tell him the whole story of what had happened. During the retelling he said not a single word and didn't even ask one question, but when I was finally through he actually laughed really hard. I could hear him laughing so hard that I actually heard the old man spit a few times as he laughed.

Once he was finally finished laughing, I asked him what the hell he thought was so funny. "You are just like me when I was younger," he replied. "Even though I was clearly on the path of being a medicine man, when I was your age I still did a lot of dumb things, but now I know that the greatest lessons sometimes come from the events that seem so bad in the moment that they happen—and this is one of those moments for you. I am staying with some friends outside of Tucson, and I want you to come here right away. Call this number when you get to Tucson, and my friends will tell you how to find me."

He hung up the phone, and I was left just sitting there in disbelief. Fire Hawk was only about a two-and-a-half-hour drive from me and just after my disgraceful actions had summoned me to see him. All I could think of is how crazy life could be sometimes. Fire Hawk loved to travel but spent most of his time in South Dakota. To have him here, so close to where I lived in Arizona, just at the time of one of the lowest moments of my life, was not so unexpected as it was scary. Everything Fire Hawk did had a purpose, and usually his methods were not subtle, to say the least.

I made quick arrangements for a friend to stay and take care of my dog while I was away before I packed a small bag and headed for Tucson. When I arrived close to the town, I called the number and was directed to a place just outside Saguaro National Park. The sun was beginning to set and I was happy for the light, because this place was in a remote location. I also was glad I had a four-wheel-drive truck, because I had to travel for more than twenty miles on a rough dirt road filled with cattle crossings, boulders, arroyos, and almost impassable climbs and descents.

When I finally arrived, Fire Hawk was standing outside a small house surrounded by gardens and flowers. There was no light except for the faint flicker of a candle inside the house. I parked my truck, and he greeted me warmly. He seemed older and more frail physically than the last time I had seen him, but his smile and eyes glowed even stronger.

"We must begin right away with your healing work, James, because it's going to be very strenuous," he told me as he put his arm around my shoulders and led me into the small, shacklike house. With a knot in my stomach of not knowing what to expect, he sat me down on a chair in an almost empty room lit only by one candle sitting on what looked to be a workbench on the other side of the room.

"You must work on your emotions of anger, James," Fire Hawk began as he stood leaning against the workbench. "I was a little surprised to hear of the recent altercation you had with your neighbor, especially because of how well you handled a similar situation years ago, the day we met, and of course because of all the work you have done on yourself and for others. But these things always happen for a good reason, and that's why you are here with me now. In my tradition, when someone kills another, either by choice or accident, or when someone gets in a fight, we have a special ceremony to invoke peace in that person."

I was about ready to argue that I did have peace and that this incident was totally unlike me and would never happen again. But I knew it would be futile to argue with Fire Hawk, and deep down I knew that whatever it was he was going to do to me would help my growth as a person, so I kept my mouth shut.

Fire Hawk then turned to the bench and picked up a bundle that looked to be wrapped in deer skin. He carefully removed the hide and handed me a most unexpected item. It was a slab of red stone about ten inches long, six inches wide, and four inches deep. I turned it around in my hands and examined it as best I could in the dim light, but I saw nothing remarkable about it, although it did have an almost eerie feeling of aliveness for a simple piece of stone. After holding it for a while and Fire Hawk not saying anything, I looked up at him and was about to ask him what I was to do with it when he began his explanation.

"What you are holding is one of the most sacred things to all my people—in fact, to many Native tribes. It is a piece of precious pipestone from what is now called Pipestone National Monument in Minnesota. The rock has been used by Native peoples for thousands of years in the making of sacred healing pipes. The rock is red because it is the hardened blood of our ancestors. Up until the mid-1800s, when the white government broke the treaties they had made with us, all the various tribes would go there to that special place and dig for the precious red pipestone. Now they only let a few Indians go there at a time, and we have to be put on lists and sometimes wait many years to get permission to dig for the stone.

"The sacred place of the pipestone is right in the middle of ancestral Sioux land. That land of my ancestors was once a great sea of tall native grasses and buffalo. Now only one percent of the grasses remain and the buffalo are all dead, except for a few that the tourists stare at. The Pipestone National Monument now has white man's grass that is cut with machines and fed with sprinklers. There are exhibits that supposedly explain our traditions, with electric speakers in them so the visitors there can hear the history of our sacred place through the interpretation of the white man, who has little idea of the sacredness of the place. To us this is insulting. The place of the pipestone quarry was so sacred that in the past, various tribes that were mortal enemies would lay down their weapons and quarry the stone side by side in peace. That is one reason the pipes became known as peace pipes. The other reason is that when my people and many other tribes signed the treaties with the white government to ensure our ancestral lands, we always smoked the pipe to seal the deal we were making with them. For us, when you give your word to the pipe and smoke it, your word can never be broken. You can never break a promise with the pipe, or you will die. The white man smoked the pipe with us, but then they broke their promise. They took our lands and they turned the pipestone quarry into an amusement park.

"But they still let a few of us go there every year to quarry. We have a new treaty with them, a treaty that benefits their government. But even with all this recent history, the pipestone is still one of our most sacred possessions, and even though you are not Indian, I believe it is your time to have your own peace pipe in order to make peace with yourself and the healing of others."

A tear ran down my cheek as Fire Hawk explained all this to me. All of a sudden, I realized what an awesome thing I was holding, and I didn't feel worthy at all. I wanted to give it back to him. But just then he told me to come over to the workbench, and he lit a kerosene lantern. There were various tools laid out, and among them were a hacksaw, metal files, drill bits, and sandpaper.

"This is where you are going to make your peace pipe, with my help. But first you need to get pure and say prayers over the sacred stone."

He then led me out to the back door, and some 100 yards away I could see a fire burning and some men standing around in the firelight. We walked over to the fire, and Fire Hawk introduced me to five medicine men from different Native cultures whom he had gathered for the ceremony of the sweat lodge, which was already built and ready. I'm not going to go into the details of the sweat lodge ceremony here, but suffice it to say it was intense. While inside the sweat lodge, we all smoked from Fire Hawk's sacred pipe, and all the medicine men and myself blew smoke onto my piece of pipestone and invoked prayers of peace into it.

After the sweat lodge, we walked to a small house nearby where some women had prepared food for everyone, and we all ate a hardy meal. Since it was not yet very late, Fire Hawk said we should begin the making of my pipe while I was still purified by the sweat, and so just the two of us walked back to the workshop.

He had me lay my stone on the workbench and grabbed a thick pencil from one of the shelves above it. "First, we must draw the outline of your pipe on the stone so you can cut the raw dimensions," he explained. "Since you are not married and have no children of your own, your pipe will have the bowl at the end of the pipe. If you have your own family one day, the bowl will be near but not all the way to the end; this signifies your commitment to your family. Someday, when you have children, you will need to make another pipe."

Fire Hawk then took out his long knife from its sheath and told me how to use the straight edge of the knife to draw the outline of my pipe onto the stone's surface. After that was done, to my surprise he said, "Now use this hacksaw and cut on the lines through the rock in order to start your pipe."

Suddenly, I realized how much work this was actually going to be. It was just a simple, ordinary hacksaw normally used for cutting plastic or maybe small pieces of metal pipe. I couldn't imagine using it to cut through a four-inch-thick piece of rock multiple times to carve out the shape of the pipe. Fire Hawk must have seen my expression and said, "Nowadays, many people use electric tools and grinders to make and sell pipes, but that is too easy and not the sacred way. You must make yours only by using these hand tools. Then your pipe will have true power from your sweat and determination."

He handed me a clamp to attach to the bench and onto my stone to prevent it from moving too much as I sawed. Then he pulled up a chair and watched intently as I began to saw into the rock. It was extremely difficult but actually not quite as hard as I thought. He could tell what I was thinking and casually commented, "That is why we purify always in the sweat lodge first before we do anything of importance. If you had not done your purifying and said your prayers to the sacred stone, you wouldn't have a chance in hell of cutting it with a simple hacksaw."

Well, I guess he was right, because within an hour I had completed my first horizontal cut that would eventually be the front edge of the pipe stem. "You did well," he said with a smile. "Since I am your sponsor in this, I will help you now by making the next cut as you rest your hands awhile."

I had to admit that my hands and arms were burning and could use a break. Fire Hawk told me to make some prayer bundles of tobacco and small pieces of cloth while he cut, because using my hands in that simple fashion would keep them from getting knotted up, and also I would need the prayer bundles when we did the initial ceremony with the completed pipe the next night. Fire Hawk had instructed me years before on how to make the bundles, and he had all the materials laid out on a small table next to the bench where I could sit in a chair and work.

The cut he made for me was the longest one of the pipe and went from the tip to the end of the bowl. I guess I wasn't surprised that the frail old man took about half the time to make a cut twice as long as the one I did. After all, he was a medicine man.

In the end, we made a total of six cuts to make the crude shape of what was to be my peace pipe. Even as roughly hewn as it was in that moment, I still remember how exquisitely beautiful it was. Even though my hands and arms were burning with fatigue, when I held it in my hands it felt like I was making love to the gods.

"I'm glad you feel the power beginning to emerge from your pipe, but there is much work to be done yet until you really feel what I am trying to teach you. Take your stone and go to sleep now. Just near the sweat lodge there is a small hogan, prepared for you by the women here that fed you. There are blankets and pillows and water. Place the stone under your pillow before you sleep. When the sun rises, I will meet you at the house where we ate earlier and we will have some food. Bring your stone, of course, because tomorrow we finish your pipe."

The dawn came quickly, and although I hadn't slept much, I felt refreshed and ready for the work that lay ahead. But as I removed my half-made stone pipe from under my pillow, I suddenly felt a little remorse because I thought by Fire Hawk telling me to put it under my pillow that I would have had some kind of special dreams or visions or something, but none of that happened. However, something special did happen. As I was ready to leave the hogan with my stone and enter into the daylight, I felt a sudden apprehension that my stone was naked and that it should be covered. I looked around, and right next to the exit/entrance of the hogan was a piece of deer pelt and a colorful handwoven piece of cloth of the same size that fit perfectly to wrap my new pipe in. Someone had delivered them in the night. I had a pretty good guess who it was.

But as is often the case when dealing with powerful medicine men, I was wrong. During breakfast, I kept catching the eye of an old lady that seemed to be the oldest person there. I felt compelled to watch her every move, but that would be disrespectful, so I only made small glances her way, and she said not a word to me. I had the feeling she spoke little English but that was not why she didn't talk to me.

After breakfast, Fire Hawk and I went back to the workshop with my wrapped bundle, and I asked him about it. "You were gifted last night by the grandmother that keeps the most holy pipe of this land," he replied. "She made that bundle for you on a vision that someone was coming here to make a pipe, just as I had the same vision, and that's why I brought the stone here. Neither of us knew at the time that it would be you. But nonetheless, we both were prepared for this pipe making by the Great Spirit, so consider yourself blessed.

"This next part will be the most challenging, as now you need to drill the holes for both the pipe stem and the bowl." I unwrapped the raw pipe, and Fire Hawk placed it vertically into the vice and handed me a small steel drill bit. He also handed me a pair of work gloves that had rubber on the palms.

With a grin, he said, "Back in ancient times, the maker of the pipe would bleed during this part, as he put his hands on either side of a stone bit and rubbed back and forth on the bit to create the holes for many hours or even days. But we can cheat just a little and use steel and gloves. The most important thing is that you still do it by hand and not machine.

"You must be very attentive to use the bit to create a straight hole all the way through the length of the stem to the base of the pipe bowl."

I did as he said, and for many hours I rubbed the bit back and forth to create the hole through the stem. Then he gave me some spring water and a larger bit, and I drilled it through the bowl, into the stem.

"Come outside into the sun, my son, and blow through the pipe for the first time."

Walking out into the sun, Fire Hawk told me to raise the pipe to the sun and say my prayers of peace, to send my anger into Father Sun. As I did that, I felt a sudden release, like my whole human organism—all my past-life experiences of anger and confusion—were blown into the ether.

With that done, we walked back inside and he showed me with patience and vigilance how to use the files and various grades of sandpaper to shape the rounded edges of my pipe.

Right about the time the sun was setting, my pipe was complete. Fire Hawk had made many more prayer bundles while I worked, and he seemed very satisfied when I handed him my pipe for final inspection.

After all that work, I was famished, but when we went back to the house and I expected to eat, there was no food. The old woman, the sacred pipe keeper, was sitting at the table, smoking a hand-rolled cigarette. All she did was stand up and place in my hand a small amount of ground cornmeal while she stared into my eyes.

Then she walked me out of the house with Fire Hawk behind us and led us to the sweat lodge. The medicine men were already there; the fire heating the sacred stones of the lodge were already heated. The old woman entered the lodge first, walked clockwise inside and sat down next to the entrance. The medicine men followed and sat in a circle with their backs against the walls of the lodge.

Fire Hawk was the fire keeper that night and brought in the heated stones one by one with a forked cedar limb. As the lodge heated up quickly and I began to sweat profusely, the old woman unfurled her sacred pipe and handed it to me in my left hand. She then instructed me to place my new pipe in my right hand.

"These pipes represent everything that we are, young man," she said. "They are the tools that help us to touch God, the Great Spirit. Without them, we have nothing. You are now a holder of a sacred pipe that will give you peace and help you spread that peace to all you meet."

We smoked first from her pipe and then from mine, passing each to the left but placing each in the right hand of the person beside us. It was one of the most special moments in my life.

We did five rounds of smoking each pipe while all the medicine men chanted sacred prayers. I was in such an ecstatic and altered state I actually don't recall what I sang, but I know I was singing too.

After the lodge was over, Fire Hawk sent me home with only a few spoken words.

About a year or so later, I found out that Fire Hawk had died. I didn't go to his funeral because no one knew how to find me, so I don't even know exactly what they did with him when he died, and I never asked. The only reason I even knew about his death was because I kept trying to contact him to no avail, until one day a man answered the phone at a gas station near the trading post in South Dakota where Fire Hawk had lived. It was one of the medicine men who had been in the lodge and had helped me bless my pipe.

He told me to come there, and the next week I did. I tried not to cry on the drive from my home to Fire Hawk's reservation, but I still did several times. I couldn't believe he was actually gone from this physical world.

I went directly to the house of the old woman who held the sacred pipe. She led me to Fire Hawk's favorite place atop a high hill. But there was no gravesite there. When I asked about it, she just shook her head at me.

"Here is where Fire Hawk's spirit flew. Here is where you honor him. The way you do that is to break your pipe in half and leave it here. Then someday you will make another pipe and remember all he taught you. That is the way we remember and pass down our tradition."

I broke my pipe and laid it on the hill where Fire Hawk had flown away. I have yet to make another one, but someday I will. Since the making of my peace pipe with Fire Hawk, I have never even thought about having another physical altercation with anyone.

———•◆•———

Engaging the Flow

One of my last lessons while apprenticing with Maggie came as an exceptionally big surprise. She sat Amy and me down on the bench outside of her lab. "I have a very special errand for you," Maggie said in a mysterious voice that told me right away that she was going to drop another one of her bombs on me (us). "Once a year since the day the water shamans saved my life when I was around your age, I have traveled back to a sacred spring in Hawaii where the water shamans live, to renew my connection to the water spirits. For the last fifteen years since I bought this property, I have been bringing water from the sacred spring in Hawaii back here to bless the land every year. It is part of a special offering and commitment that I have made with the spirits. This year, I want you two to go for me—that is, if you would like to."

Amy and I were both extremely excited, and neither of us had ever been to Hawaii. "Now, wait—before you get too excited," Maggie quickly added. "I'm sure you'll have a few days to enjoy yourself, but the main mission of this trip is to visit the sacred spring and bring back with you a container of water from the spring to give to the soil of this land. It's not going to be an easy task. The spring is in a remote and secluded area. It will be difficult to reach and maybe even dangerous, since you are not familiar with the land and the *kakayeri* spirits (the protectors of sacred places) will be watching you.

"Your task on this trip is to test your seeing by finding the sacred spring. I've sworn an oath to never reveal its location, so the two of you are going to have to find it yourselves. The only thing I can tell you is that it's located within one of the Hawaiian islands. Other than that, you guys are on your own."

Amy and I looked at each other, and for the first time since I'd known her, I saw a tinge of apprehension or even fear on her face. She was the most confident person I'd ever met, but the news of this test that Maggie had just sprung on us had gotten her a little rattled.

"You're going to want to travel light. No extra luggage or unnecessary baggage," Maggie continued. "In the lab, you'll find one backpack for each of you. The backpacks are big enough to carry what you need but small enough to be brought onto the plane as a carry-on. I've put a few essential supplies in the packs for you already. The only other things you'll need are some clothes. I will give you a small amount of cash and a credit card so you can get around and buy food, but no amount of money will help you find the spring. For that, you'll have to enter into the flow of the islands."

Maggie looked at the both of us. Neither of us said anything, so Maggie went on.

"Getting into the flow means raising your level of awareness to what is going on around you and then allowing the situations you are in to unfold naturally, without trying to control or guide them one way or the other. It's anticipating and following what appear to be coincidences and synchronistic events. It's opening to see the opportunities presented to you when they arise. If you engage the flow, the sacred spring will draw you in naturally. Just like the sacred garden of this land, which both of you found in a very special way through your seeing, the sacred spring will also be silently calling to you once you are in Hawaii. If you are open enough to feel the pull of the sacred place, then the place will guide you to it."

Amy's expression had totally changed. Her old confident self had returned. She had a look of total concentration on her face, and she was silently nodding her head in agreement to what Maggie was explaining. Seeing Amy's expression raised my confidence level immediately, even though I still had no idea how in the world we were ever going to the find the spring.

"Can you tell us anything more about the sacred spring?" I asked Maggie. "What makes it so special?"

"That's a good question. On a physical level, the spring is located on a lush tropical island that is teeming with life in the middle of the ocean. It is a young place that is still being formed by the active volcanoes that make up the islands. It's a place where lava, the fiery heart of the land, joins with the ocean, the salty water of creation. It's a place that is literally bursting with life. And when the water of that youthfully spirited place is fed to the soil of this ancient land, it miraculously invigorates the soil with lively and vibrant energy. But that's only half of the story.

"The other half is about the energy of human intent. I have been making the trip to the sacred spring for all these years because my trip represents an offering that clearly demonstrates my willingness to acknowledge, and to remain connected to, the natural cycles of life through honoring the cycles of water. The rain, oceans, rivers, springs, clouds, sky, and the sun—they all drive the sacred cycles of water that provide us with life. By using my energy to honor these cycles, I place myself inside of them, and they honor me back by providing me with deep feelings of peace and well-being, not to mention the life-giving water for my gardens and trees to grow. It takes a lot of time and effort to make the trip to the sacred spring each year, but it is exactly the time and effort spent that gives strength and power to my offering. The intent and the reverence included in my offering also adds power to the water of the sacred spring when I pour it into the soil of this land."

As I gazed at Maggie's land, I had to admit that whatever she was doing was obviously working. The lawns, the gardens, the orchard—even the insects and the birds and all the other creatures—were extraordinarily vigorous and healthy. It was also obvious that bringing the water from the sacred spring back to her land was something extremely important to Maggie on a deeply personal level, and I felt honored that she was allowing Amy and me to make the trip for her this time. I just hoped that we wouldn't let her down.

During the days approaching the trip, Amy and I spent all of our free time studying the geography and the plant and animal life of the Hawaiian islands. Maggie thought it was a prudent thing to do, but she also made it clear that it wouldn't help us much in finding the spring. She said that map-making and reading books about flora and fauna were activities of the rational mind, but finding the sacred spring would require our rational thoughts to be quieted and our hearts to be open to feel the pull of the sacred place.

The following few days after we left were a whirlwind. We arrived in Hawaii, and in a wake of synchronistic events placed before us, we arrived one day at a secluded beach. What happened next I could never have fathomed: Amy and I were split up. While I was surfing, she got lost (not typical for Amy) in the tropical forest while hiking, and I was knocked unconscious by a giant wave.

I awoke to the sound of cascading water, but it definitely wasn't the ocean. I was lying on my back, and when I opened my eyes there was nothing but blue sky above me. I sat up slowly and was stunned by what I saw.

I stared in wonderment all around me. I was no longer at the beach; I was somewhere deep in the tropical jungle, and I was on a raft made of reeds, floating in the center of a large pool of water at the base of a tall waterfall. It was like a scene right out of a movie.

Despite the sheer beauty of the place, I was all alone, and that worried me immediately because I had no idea where I was or where Amy was. Obviously, someone had brought me there and put me on the raft, but whoever they were, they were nowhere in sight. I felt horrible. My mouth tasted like a combination of puke and saltwater. My pack was lying at my feet, so the first thing I decided to do was brush my teeth. I went into my pack and discovered that sitting next to it was a small wooden container filled with water and a small plate with slices of pineapple and papaya on it.

I brushed my teeth and then drank some of the water. As I ate a few slices of fruit and pondered what to do next, I heard someone approaching from the shore behind me. A young woman appeared from the jungle and stood at the edge of the pool about twenty yards from me. She seemed to be slightly older than me, and from her appearance there seemed no doubt that she was a native Hawaiian. During my stay in that magical place, Kani and I would become lifelong friends.

The first thing I asked Kani about was Amy. "I don't know where your friend is," Kani replied. "But I have been told that our people are watching her so that she is kept safe while she tries to find you or the spring or both. This situation is not something that can be easily explained. For whatever reason, the water spirit has delivered you here, but your friend must arrive here on her own. That is her task. If she does not find this place by the time you are ready to leave, then my people will take you to her. But for now, your place is here. The water shamans of my people, Lauwa and Awaul, have invited you to participate in a sacred ceremony, since it seems the water spirit has summoned you here."

"Kani, what do you mean the water spirit summoned me here? I don't even remember how I got here. Can you tell me what happened?"

"Of course I can tell you," Kani replied. "It's very simple, really. The water shaman Awaul felt something stirring in the waters of what some people call Coral Reef, and he sent two of the seers of our village to go and find out what was going on. They were in the forest above the beach while you were surfing. They watched you and your friend there for a while and didn't notice anything special. But they continued to wait and saw your friend leave you. She walked straight toward them as if she had sensed or seen that they were there. At that moment, they knew that she was a young seer, so they thought that was the reason why the shaman had sent them to that beach. One of the seers, the female, followed your friend to see what she was up to, and the other seer, the male, stayed watching you. That's when he saw the face of the water spirit in the giant wave you were riding, and the next thing he knew, the wave had swallowed you and then spit you out onto the beach like a sour grape.

"You were unconscious and full of water. If the seer hadn't been there, you probably would have died. He went to you and helped your body expel the water in your lungs, and you threw up everything in your stomach as well. When you started breathing again, he tried to wake you, but you were still under the spell of the water spirit, and the seer knew that he had to take you to Awaul and Lauwa to be cured. He carried you on his back all the way here to the village, and then the shamans worked on you. They discovered there was nothing really wrong with you. The water spirit simply wanted you to come here as soon as possible, and sometimes the water spirit can be very harsh in its methods. So, following the water spirit's wishes, they put you on the raft in the middle of the pool, where they knew you would in time wake up."

I was dumbfounded. "But what about Amy?" I asked.

"The female seer, Kawani, is secretly watching over her on her journey. Your friend now has two tasks: to find you and to find the sacred spring. You must try to put her from your mind right now. You have your own lessons to learn here in our village."

Later, as the sun was setting and after meeting lots of people, I noticed a crowd forming and went to investigate. There was an old man kneeling on the ground, dressed in an elaborate outfit with colorful embroidery of animals and birds and various symbols, who was beginning to light a fire. Just before lighting it, he looked up into the crowd and motioned me to help him.

"You must have a special connection to the fire," Kani said to me after we lit the fire and I rejoined the crowd. "It's not his habit to invite strangers to help him light the sacred fire."

"I'm just as surprised as you are," I said. "It was an amazing experience. Who is that old guy?"

"He's a Huichol shaman from the mountains of Mexico," she replied. "His name is Nichu, and he's an elder that sings the voice of Grandfather Fire."

"So what's he doing here?" I asked.

Kani looked at me for a moment as if she was surprised by my question. She took a deep breath and said, "This is a sacred place; it has been a part of the native Hawaiian tradition for longer than anyone can remember. During the last few decades, many people from all over the world have been guided to this sacred place—not just here, but also to sacred sites all over the world. Sacred sites like this one are bursting with energy, with life force. In general, people are drawn to sacred sites mostly because they can see and feel the beauty or the unique quality of the place. But shamans and seers make pilgrimages to these kinds of places to make offerings and to work with the spirits that give life to the sacred site. For example, the fire shaman Nichu comes here on a pilgrimage to the sacred spring at least once every five years to work with the youthful spirit of the water that lives here, and the water shamans Awaul and Lauwa go on pilgrimage to the mountains where Nichu lives to work with the ancient spirit of the fire that lives there. Sometimes, when people come here, they end up staying for weeks, months, or even years. That's one of the things that makes this place so special. In this village, we have shamans and seers from many different cultures living and working together. The day after tomorrow, shamans and seers from all over the world will be coming here on their pilgrimage to the waters of the sacred spring. Your teacher has been coming here every year since I was a little girl."

"You know Maggie?" I asked in surprise.

"Of course. I've known her my whole life. But here she is known by the name she was given by the water spirit. Here she is known as Magpie."

After the evening meal, I was introduced to the water shamans. Both were enormous and very round in shape. Both had dark hair and skin, with shiny, penetrating eyes. I had the distinct impression that they might be twins, but earlier Kani had told me about Awaul and Lauwa. "They are powerful shamans who know the magic of the water spirit. They met when they were children, and they have been together ever since. They are husband and wife, but they are also so much more that I can't even really explain it. The only thing I can say is that together they are the water."

"Can you explain what you mean by that?" I asked, perplexed.

"I can try," replied Kani. "Awaul is the male shaman. He is the clouds, fog, thunder, and rain. His counterpart is Lauwa. She is also a water shaman, but she is the streams, rivers, lakes, and oceans. Awaul is the water that moves through the air, and Lauwa is the water that flows on the ground. They are opposites, yet they are the same. They complement each other and make each other whole. Shamans of some cultures call them shapeshifters, because they can appear to you in a variety of ways, depending on how they want you to see them. Sometimes they appear young, other times old, and sometimes in a completely different form. At times it's hard to tell them apart, as one may do the job of the other, so you are unaware of who is who. They are magical beings, but their magic isn't done with tricks. Their magic comes from a lifetime of learning how to connect to the life force of the water. Here in the village they are shamans. They are healers who help to keep the balance between the human beings living here and the natural world that we are part of. They help people learn how to be fluid in body and mind, to see things from different perspectives, to grow into their full human potential."

Together, the shamans suggested that I spend the night on the raft in the center of the sacred pool below the waterfall, instead of in the bed of the hut that Kani had shown me. They told me that sleeping on the raft in the middle of the lagoon would give me a chance to connect and acquaint myself with the water spirit. If I spoke to the water spirit, introduced myself, and let the water spirit know that I had traveled very far to be there, in the morning I might have a special surprise waiting for me. Then, without another word, Awaul and Lauwa turned and vanished into the mist.

"Come on, grab your sleeping mat," Kani said excitedly. "I'll walk down to the pool with you and make sure you're all set. Have you ever slept on the water?"

I grabbed the sleeping mat, and as we walked down the trail I admitted to Kani that this would be my first time sleeping on the water.

Kani waited by the shore while I paddled my raft out to the middle of the sacred pool and secured it to one of the underwater posts. She then waved goodbye, and I was alone. Feeling tired from all that had happened recently, I doubted that I would have any trouble falling asleep, even on a raft in the middle of a lake. I lay back on the raft and stared up into the bright night sky full of stars and moonlight from an almost-full moon.

I felt peaceful and content and was almost asleep when I suddenly remembered what the water shamans had suggested that I do. I stood up and thought about how I should introduce myself to the water spirit. I felt awkward and rather silly that I was actually about to talk to water. I silently wished to myself that Amy were there; she would be so much better at this than me. But, I figured, what the heck—and I began to speak in a strong voice out across the water.

"Spirit of the water: if you can hear me, Lauwa and Awaul said it would be a good idea for me to introduce myself to you. My name is James. I have come a long way to be with you and to find the sacred spring so that I can take some of your water back home with me for my teacher's garden." Not knowing what else to say, I paused for a few seconds, then continued. "You probably know my teacher; her name is Maggie—or Magpie, I guess, is what they call her here. She is an awesome woman. Anyway, thank you for listening to me. I hope I get the chance to meet you. Good night."

After my little speech, I felt almost proud of myself that I actually had done it. Boy, was I a different person than I used to be, I thought to myself as I lay back down on the raft. If any of my old friends back home would have seen that speech, they would think I had gone right over the deep end. But I knew in my heart it was the right thing to do. Plus, I was now on the turf of the water shamans, and they knew best what and what not to do here. With all the recent talk of kakayeri and malicious spirits, I was happy to just follow the shamans' advice and then go to sleep.

When I awoke, I was in the middle of a sea of fog. I could barely see two feet in front of me, and I wondered how I was going to make it to the shore. Looking around me, I noticed that another raft was attached to the back of mine. I carefully climbed onto it. It seemed to be much bigger than the one I had spent the night on. I crawled a few feet forward and bumped right into a giant leg. It was Awaul. He was standing there on the raft, and next to him was Lauwa. Awaul extended a hand to me and helped me to stand up. I couldn't see the whole raft, but it was obviously large and strong enough to hold the three of us stable on the water. I thought to myself that it must be tied to the other posts I had seen the day before.

"Good morning, James," the shamans said together.

"You awoke just in time to receive a gift from the water spirit," Lauwa added. "We are facing east, waiting for the sunlight to add its magic to the morning."

The ambient light gradually began to grow, and the fog began to clear into a light mist so that it was possible to barely see the shoreline. The sunlight grew stronger, and a slight breeze sent the mist swirling gently around us. Standing on the raft in the middle of the pool and swirling mist felt like we were standing in the clouds. I felt like I was in a dream and that we were floating gently through the air.

Lauwa told me to look out and to try to take in the whole scene in front of me. She told me to open my mind and my heart and to try to see the wheel of water flowing. At first I didn't understand what she wanted me to do. I continued to stand there with them, and Lauwa began to softly chant, repeating a simple verse.

> *The water flows as the lifeblood of the world.*
> *The water flows as the lifeblood of the world.*
> *The water flows as the lifeblood of the world.*

A few refrains later, she motioned me to join her, and I began to chant the verse with her. As we continued to sing, Awaul joined in chanting a different verse.

"Sun inspires water to rise floating to the sky," Awaul chanted. And after a few refrains, he motioned for me to join him.

For the next few minutes, Awaul and Lauwa alternated verses, with me chanting them both. Then Lauwa added another verse:

> *Clouds gather to release rain to the ground.*

I chanted the three verses with them.

A few minutes later, Awaul added the concluding verse, and the three of us repeated the whole chant many times while alternating the verses between us:

The water flows as the lifeblood of the world
Sun inspires water to rise floating to the sky
Clouds gather to release rain to the ground
The children of water drink happily another day

In the middle of the misty pool, the meaning of the song gradually sunk into my heart and something opened up inside of me. I suddenly stood facing the flowing wheel of water. The great wheel was the endless cycle of transformation that the water continuously makes. It flows, floats, falls, and nurtures in an eternal journey that brings life to the world.

I'm not sure how long the three of us stood there chanting in front of the great wheel of water, but when the final verse was over, the mist was gone, the rain had stopped, and the sun was shining brightly onto the pool, creating reflections of the shore and sky. I desperately wanted to get into the water. Awaul whispered to me that it was okay, and I slowly slipped in. Underwater, with my eyes open, I looked around and saw that the flowing aliveness that was in the wheel of water was now all around me. I felt a peacefulness fill my body, and I floated effortlessly in the water while still looking in wonder at what I was seeing. I felt like I could feel the whole body of water—that my body and its body were the same, and the water was just as alive as I was.

Gradually, I began to see that the life of the pool seemed to be somehow flowing in from a place on the other side of the pool at the base of the waterfall. It was like that place was the heart that pumped life into the pool the same way my heart pumped blood through my veins. I felt drawn to the place by the waterfall and swam in that direction. When I reached the waterfall, I stood up and let the water rain down on my head and shoulders. It felt great, like a massage of water. I peered into the area behind the waterfall and saw that there was a large cave. As I stepped into the cave, my jaw dropped. The cave had no floor. Instead, there was a pool of cool, clear water that seemed to radiate a faint light of the same colorful non-color that I had seen underwater. Without a shadow of a doubt, I knew that I had found the sacred spring.

I dove in and swam joyously under the water. The feeling of life force was astounding. The water felt as alive as any plant or animal I had ever touched or petted. When I emerged, I heard a familiar voice behind me say, "Well done, young seer."

Awaul and Lauwa had followed me and were standing, facing me, with their backs to the waterfall. "Magpie will be very proud of you," Lauwa said, smiling. "But more importantly, you were able to quiet your thoughts and open up to seeing and feeling the spirit of the water. You let your consciousness flow out, and you were able to see how the water is constantly transforming and moving from land to sky and back again like a giant wheel that spins into eternity.

"Now your next challenge will be to put the knowledge of your meeting with the water spirit to work. For knowledge gained through seeing is useless if it doesn't help us to grow. The point of you meeting the water spirit has been for you to learn to become more fluid in your thoughts and actions."

Amy also made it to the sacred spring in her own way, but that is another story...

<hr />

First Flight

One morning, Nichu[1] entered my hut before dawn and told me we had a special task that day.

"Very soon there will be an important festival here in the village, and many people from villages all throughout the mountains will come. I need some new feathers for my muvieri and to make prayer arrows. I will climb high among the rocky cliffs where the eagle and hawk nest. I understand you are a good climber?"

---

1 Nichu is not only a Huichol shaman but also a *kawitero*, which roughly translates to an elder who holds the knowledge of the tradition. They are usually elder men who have spent their whole lives in spiritual practice. While shamans are not uncommon in Huichol society, kawiteros are. In some places, there is only one kawitero for many villages. To be working directly with a kawitero was an enormous honor for me.

"You bet!" I replied happily as the excitement of going climbing made my skin tingle and muscles tense.

It's not easy to keep up with a Huichol walking in his mountains, even one who's over eighty years old. From their first years of life, these people walk everywhere they go, and after a lifetime of walking it could easily be said that Nichu was an expert. I was totally embarrassed more than once that the old man had to stop and wait for me to catch up. He just laughed and said that for a *tewari,* I was doing better than he expected. I no longer took offense to the term tewari, or gringo. In most cases, the Huichol simply used those words to signify a person who was not Huichol, but not in a derogatory way.

After long hours of hiking the trails in that isolated region of the Sierra Madres in western Mexico, we finally reached the base of the cliffs high above Nichu's village. They were sheer and perfect for the technical climbing I was used to. The only problem was we weren't carrying any ropes or safety gear. When I questioned Nichu about it, all he said was, "You can stay here if you like. I'm going up."

I figured he must have done this lots of times before and probably knew the easiest way up. I was an excellent climber, and if I took the same route up as he did, I was confident I'd be all right. Walking in the mountains was one thing, but I was sure I had more strength for climbing than old Nichu did.

The first part of the climb was brutal, and by the time we finally stopped to rest on a thin ledge, my hands and arms were burning, and my calves ached in pain. Nichu wasn't even breathing hard. As I sat there resting, I surveyed the next section above us, and it didn't look half as difficult. There were even a few trees growing on the rocky slope. Nichu commented that I was doing well and explained that the next section was just a short hike, not really climbing, but then the last section was the most difficult and that I should try and stay right behind him so I could see which hand and foot holds to use as we went up.

We strode easily up the second section, and before starting to climb the sheer wall that was now in front of us, Nichu and I drank some water and took a small swig of *tejuino,* the sacred corn beverage, "for strength."

Nichu rocketed up the rock face and I tried my best to keep up, but it was no use—he was too strong and fast. After a few minutes, he was way up above me and eventually disappeared from my view. I continued to climb at my own pace and found adequate hand and foot holds. My only fear stemmed from the fact that I had never climbed that high before without ropes and safety gear.

Eventually, I came to a section that rock climbers call "the crux." The crux is the most difficult part of any climb, usually a blank face of rock or a roof section that has only one set of moves to get past it. This crux was a sheer section of rock; the only hold at all was a tiny horizontal crack about a foot higher than I could reach. If somehow I could get above that crack, the area above it looked like it had plenty of holds and I'd be okay. So I decided to take a chance. I'd jump for the crack, "smear" my feet up, and reach for the bigger holds above.

Everything went as planned and I was feeling very proud of myself when I suddenly noticed that the section above me was not at all as it had looked from below. Above me was another sheer face of rock. Luckily, as I scanned the area, I noticed that to the right, near the corner of the cliff, there was a roof section that looked fairly easy—well, easy as roofs go. Roofs are large overhangs that usually require you to either climb upside down and horizontal to the cliff or let go with your feet.

I climbed up to the roof and surveyed it. It stretched about four feet back over my head but there were some decent holds in the rock. I nailed the first two hand holds, got a good foot, and was just about to jut over the lip of the roof when I heard a dreaded sound: rattlesnake. The top of the roof was probably a perfect place for a sunbathing snake. Now I was in trouble. If the snake was already annoyed and rattling, I couldn't afford to place a blind hand up onto the lip of the roof, but I had already committed to the move, so I was hanging horizontal to the roof, with nowhere to go.

I couldn't go up, it was impossible for me to go back without falling, and I couldn't hang on much longer in the awkward position I was in.

Weighing my options quickly while basically hanging upside down, I decided that taking my chances with the snake was better than falling to my death, so I pushed off hard with my left foot and lunged up and over with my right arm. That's when things got even worse. The snake didn't strike, but there were no handholds to grab onto. I still couldn't see above the roof, so I searched blindly with my right hand above me for something to grab onto, but the rock was as smooth as a pool table.

I screamed for Nichu to help me. There was no going forward and no going back. I was hanging by one arm and had only one foot contacting the wall. I was in a complete state of panic and only moments from falling two hundred feet to my death. "How could Nichu have done this to me?" I thought. "How could he have left me alone on this cliff?" I was so pissed off and frightened of dying that in the last few seconds before I would fall, the world seemed to stop.

Everything went silent around me. Everything went silent within me. I couldn't even feel my heart beat or hear my breath. That's when I realized I had left my body. I was looking slightly down at myself hanging by one arm from the roof. And below me to the right, around the corner of the cliff, I saw two men sitting comfortably on a wide ledge. It was Nichu and Matziwa. Those bastards! They were no more than three feet away and didn't even answer my screams for help.

I was so mad, confused, and terrified all at the same time that I did something incredible: I saved my life. Somehow I communicated to myself that if I swung really hard around the corner to the right and let go at the proper moment, I would fall easily onto the wide ledge that the two men were sitting on. So that's what I did.

Screaming at the top of my lungs, I swung myself out to the corner of the cliff and let myself drop where I couldn't see. I landed right onto the wide ledge. The drop was only about three feet, which made the whole thing very anticlimactic.

The two old men were laughing so hard at my screaming entrance that they were holding their sides. That was too much for me. I stared at them for a few moments and burst out in tears. I sat down on the ledge with my head between my knees and cried. I couldn't believe what had just happened. I had almost died. And for what? Memories flooded my mind, and I remembered Matziwa years before in the principal's office telling me I shouldn't throw my life away. But the bastard was right there on this ledge when I almost died again for nothing. I wanted to go home. I wanted to see Amy. I wanted to cut the lawn at Maggie's farm. I wanted to do anything to be as far away from those two old wackos as possible.

However, that wasn't meant to be. I was trapped on the ledge with the two old shamans, end of story. They both looked me up and down with cold eyes and smiled. If I hadn't been so pissed off at them I probably would have smiled too. I mean, I wasn't dead, and that was worth smiling about. But now I had a million questions running through my mind.

"Men have to be pushed to their limit," Nichu said to me calmly before I could ask a question. "We are stubborn and don't like to change our ways. Only in times of severe stress or danger will we let loose our full potential. Now women, they are different. They have that incredible opening between their legs that connects them to the cycles of the world. When needed they can change at the drop of a hat, and that's why their training is sometimes much different from ours."

"Do you mean to tell me that almost *killing* me was part of my training?" I asked between clenched teeth.

"For some men it need not be so dramatic, but in your case it was necessary due to your thick head. You are very headstrong and needed a powerful jolt to make you act in a different way than you're used to. Confronting your death—a death that would have been the result of your own stupidity rather than a mere accident—proved to be sufficient in bringing out your hidden resource: your ethereal body, which we also call the traveler's body."

"Congratulations," Matziwa said as he spoke for the first time. "You have passed the test. Welcome to the world of the traveler."

I didn't know what to say. I didn't know whether to feel elated or scared out of my mind.

"You're still kind of numb," Nichu said while patting me on the back. "It takes a lot of energy to break our consciousness free from its imagined chain of the flesh and leave the body behind. But you'll get used to it. The first few years are the hardest."

"I had a good feeling about you," Matziwa added with a laugh. "That was a darn good show! Shall we collect some feathers now?"

Matziwa stood up and turned toward Nichu as if he was putting the whole incident behind him.

"Wait just a minute!" I protested loudly. "Don't I get any kind of explanation? I mean—Matziwa, what are you even *doing* here?"

"I am a Huichol, and these are my mountains. I come here when I wish. But to answer your question, I came here this time for you—to see if you would be a traveler as I had hoped. Now that I know you are able, your real training with Nichu and the other travelers can begin."

"What training is that?"

"The use of your ethereal body, of course—your traveler's body."

With that, Matziwa casually placed one foot over the edge of the cliff ledge, looked me straight in the eye, and deftly hopped off the ledge. I looked over at Nichu in horror, then ran over to where he had jumped. Peering over the ledge, I could see Matziwa standing way down at the base of the cliff, waving his arms at me. I stumbled back in disbelief and hit my back hard against the rock face. Nichu just laughed and shook his head.

The next thing I knew, Matziwa was back on the ledge with us, and I thought my head was going to burst.

"You still don't get it, do you?" Nichu commented. "Matziwa is demonstrating for you his traveler's body. He has mastered the art of letting his consciousness flow out from his body to such a high degree that he can appear to be in two places at once. This is not Matziwa's physical body that you see in front of you. You have never met Matziwa while he has been in his body. His part in your training has to do with the traveler's body, and that is what this day is all about."

"But if you aren't really here," I asked Matziwa, "where are you?"

"I am really here. But my physical body is not."

"So where is your physical body?" I countered.

"You're not ready yet for that answer," Matziwa replied. "Someday, but not today. Today we travel with the ethereal body—like you did once with an eagle. Come along now."

In one swift movement, Nichu moved behind me and grabbed me tightly around the waist while at the same time Matziwa hit me hard in the solar plexus with his fist. Instantly, I saw him standing in front of me as a sphere of energy.

"Good," I heard him say. "Let's go."

Matziwa's sphere of energy was overlapping with mine, and as he moved away I felt what I can only describe as a tug that released my energy sphere from my body. However, I could also clearly see that I wasn't completely severed from my body—there were lines, like strings of energy, attached to both my physical body and my energy sphere, which was still stuck to the energy sphere of Matziwa.

That's when Matziwa jumped from the cliff with my ethereal body. We soared all the way down and stopped gently at the bottom. The energy lines were still attached, and I could see them running all the way down the cliff to where we were standing. Then Matziwa sort of sprung upwards and the energy lines snapped us back like a rubber band, so that a few seconds later we were back on the cliff and I was seeing out of my normal eyes again.

"Now don't get any big ideas," Nichu admonished. "The only reason you are able to use your traveler's body in the way you just did is because Matziwa and I are lending you our energy. I am lending the energy to your physical body to keep it safe here on the ledge, and Matziwa is lending you his energy in order for you to travel with him. But you are not ready to do this by yourself; it takes a lot of practice, experience, and more energy than you currently possess.

"What we are doing today is simply showing you what is possible—that mind and matter truly are different waves in the same pool, and that the wave of your consciousness is not trapped in your head like a fish trapped in a fishbowl. The world is your ocean, and with enough energy, combined with sufficient skill, your consciousness can float, swim, or travel by speedboat to wherever it desires to go."

I should have been a lot more freaked out than I was by what was happening, but instead I was perfectly calm. Nichu noticed my state of mind and said that the way I was feeling was due to the extraordinary force of energy that Matziwa had used to stick me to him as we traveled down and up the cliff. Being in direct contact with Matziwa's energy had caused a radical shift in my perception, and Nichu said it was doubtful that I would even remember what happened once their lesson was over and I returned to my ordinary state of consciousness.

The two men stood next to me, and Matziwa explained that on this side of the cliff there were a series of ledges similar to the one we were standing on. When he was a kid, he and his friends used to climb up and down these cliffs so often that they knew exactly how to reach the bottom by jumping from one ledge down to another, even when they couldn't see the next ledge below them.

"That's what we're going to do!" Nichu announced in a booming voice while looking over the edge.

"But I don't know where the next ledge is," I protested.

"That's true, and that's why you're going to use your ethereal body to find out, just like you did when you made your grand entrance a little while ago. But this time Matziwa and I are going to help you so you don't do anything foolish. Since your consciousness has already left the constraints of your body twice just now, it will be easier for it to come out again, especially with us lending you our energy. The more times we can help you to pull your consciousness out now, the easier it will be for you to do by yourself when the time comes. We're kind of training it to get off the couch and walk around. For men, the ethereal body needs to be coaxed out to travel. It's rather shy."

Both of the old men laughed at Nichu's comment, and then Matziwa instructed me to sit with my back against the cliff and focus on his aura until I could see him as a sphere of energy. It didn't take long for me to see

Matziwa as a glowing sphere. He moved closer to me so that his energy engulfed me, and then he moved slowly away, and once again I felt a strange tug and I was perceiving the world from outside of my body.

"Now we're going to jump down to the next ledge together so that you can see where it is," Matziwa instructed.

We moved to the edge of the cliff and slowly went over the edge. The jump down only took a few seconds. We were on another ledge about six feet below the one Nichu and I were standing on.

"Okay. See where we are?" Matziwa asked. "We're down and a few feet to the right of where you're sitting with Nichu. Now we're going to go back up there, and then we'll all jump down to this ledge together."

Matziwa and I used the energy lines to spring back up onto the ledge. For some reason, I felt so elated that I couldn't help but tell both of them how awesome and fun this traveling out of my body stuff was. I was euphoric and wanted to jump up and down and tell the whole world what I could do.

Nichu rapped me hard on the top of my head with his knuckles. "Quit that right now," he said forcefully. "This is no game. You're feeling so happy because Matziwa is lending you his energy. You're not used to feeling so much energy. Try to control yourself and concentrate."

Nichu positioned himself in the proper place and then jumped down to the next ledge. I jumped next, then Matziwa went.

"We're going to repeat the same procedure of traveling with your ethereal body down to the next ledge and back up so you'll know exactly where it is, and then jump down with your physical body. While on each ledge, we'll also be on the lookout for the eagles and hawks that live here."

With Matziwa's help, I easily traveled with my ethereal body down to each ledge and back up again so that I could jump—or sometimes climb, depending on the steepness—down to the next ledge safely. When we got to the fourth one, which was about a third of the way down from the top where we had started, we found a huge nest. The nest was made of dry twigs interlaced one with another until they formed a perfect arrangement.

As soon as we spotted the nest, a large eagle flew down and landed on a small outcropping of rock next to the ledge, about eye level to us. Her aura was silvery and her energy strong. Matziwa gave her a quick nod of the head and the bird screeched loudly and jumped down onto the ledge, where she walked around to the back of the nest and screeched again. Nichu knelt down and reached his arm between the nest and the rock wall and pulled out four beautiful eagle feathers that were hidden there. He put them into the small bag he was carrying across his shoulders and nodded to the bird, who looked at us all quickly with many jerking motions of her head and then, as quick as she came, she was gone.

"Not long ago," Nichu said quietly, "we made an agreement with the sacred eagles here. In the old days, we used to hunt them for their feathers. The energy of the feathers is strongest when taken from a live bird. There were many eagles and hawks living in these mountains, and we never took more than we needed for our ceremonies so the birds wouldn't be afraid of us and would continue living here. But during the last fifty years, the tewaris have killed almost all of our sacred birds. We made an agreement with the birds to protect them from the tewaris if they would leave us a few of their magical feathers once in a while. That way, no one harms the birds and we still get the feathers we need."

The three of us continued down the ledges, and I pulled my ethereal body out many times to help me travel safely from one ledge to the next. By the time we reached the base of the cliff, I could easily focus on Matziwa's energy in order to "hook" mine to his and travel with him.

"Now your training with the fire can begin," Nichu said to me as we started the long walk back to the village. "You did well today; we gave your traveler's body the knowledge that it can come out. We exercised it, so to speak. The next challenge will be to convince your mind that you can travel without borrowing energy from another traveler, and that's where the fire comes in. You see, the energy of the fire is not so different from the energy of Matziwa that you used today. You can learn to use the fire in the same way to coax your ethereal body to travel outside of your head. But this you must learn on your own, without our help. The only thing we can do for you is set up the proper conditions; from there, it's all up to you."

As we reached the outskirts of the village, I suddenly noticed that Matziwa was no longer with us. I felt extremely tired and was dragging my feet by the time we reached Nichu's compound. Without even the energy to ask where Matziwa had gone, I headed straight for my bunk and fell into a deep and dreamless sleep.

I awoke the next morning to find two beautiful eagle feathers lying on my chest. Sitting up, I was aware that the sun was already bright in the sky outside the hut. "Good afternoon!" Jose Louis—one of Nichu's many sons and my best Huichol friend, who was around my same age—said to me as I left the hut to see what was going on.

Judging by the sun, I figured that it was already close to midday, and I wondered why in the world I had slept so late and why no one had woken me up. Normally I was up before dawn with everyone else. I sat down on one of the logs in the center of the compound with Jose Louis, who was busy with something in his lap. He stopped what he was doing and prepared me an instant coffee from the hot water in a pot next to the fire. I took the cup gladly and watched as he went back to work on a beautiful drawing he was making. I had seen Huichol making this type of art before, which consisted of carefully placing yarn of various colors onto a board covered with a thin layer of sticky beeswax. Jose Louis was very skilled at this, and the drawing he was making was so vibrant and intricate that it almost appeared to be alive with motion.

Noticing that I couldn't take my eyes off the drawing, Jose Louis stopped working and looked up at me. "This drawing is yours, a gift to help you on your journey. Your other gifts are in the *rirriki*, my family's temple."

I followed Jose Louis as he got up and walked over to the little hut that was the temple. I had been inside the rirriki many times, along with the rirrikis of all the other *jicareros* (men both young and old who are chosen to serve the village temple as keepers of the sacred traditions for five years) that I worked with every day. When we entered the hut, Jose Louis pointed to the left side of the altar, where a whole collection of new offerings had been set up. "When the jicareros got the news this morning, instead of going to work in the fields, they came and sat with Nichu all morning, making these prayer offerings for you."

Moving closer to the altar, I saw finely decorated arrows of wood, little muvieris, decorated gourds, candles, and many intricate yarn drawings. "But why?" I asked.

"All these things represent the prayers of the people for the safe completion of your journey. Father will be taking you after the drum ceremony that begins tomorrow and will last three days and nights."

"But where am I going?"

"Don't you know?"

"No! I haven't got a clue."

"You're going on your journey with the fire," Jose Louis said excitedly. "Now that you are a traveler, you must travel with the fire to seek your vision and find your task."

"What do you mean, now that I'm a traveler?" I asked, more confused than ever.

"Ah, I see what's going on here. You don't remember, do you?"

"Remember what?"

Just then, Nichu walked into the rirriki with four other elders. Without saying anything else, he told me to go and get the feathers I had found on my chest that morning. When I returned with the feathers, Nichu guided me to stand next to the prayer offerings the people had made for me. Then Nichu and the four other elders began blessing all the offerings, as well as my feathers and me, by chanting prayers and using the tips of their muvieris to sprinkle a small amount of water, cornmeal, and deer blood over everything.

When the blessing was finished, Nichu took the two feathers from me, tied them to a muvieri staff with a thin piece of deer sinew, and stuck the feathered muvieri into my straw hat so that the feathers pointed forward.

"These special feathers symbolize that you are a training shaman-traveler at the beginning of your journey," Nichu said in fatherly tone. "They remind the people that you are in your preparation time and not to offer you food, alcohol, sex, or anything else that might distract you. The preparation time is a time of fasting and cleansing. Four days from now, you will begin your journey."

Nichu turned to face the other elders, and all at once they shouted "Asi sera" ("So it shall be") and left the temple, patting me on the back as they went. Nichu remained, looking intensely at me. "No food or drink except water for you until your journey," Nichu said. "Because of your fast, you must not participate in the drum ceremony, where there will be food, drink, and peyote cactus. Tomorrow, before dawn, you will leave the village and camp alone in these mountains until the festival is over. When you return, you will spend five days in the *kaliway* (sacred temple) to learn how to travel with the fire. Understand?"

"Yes," I replied nervously. "But why is this all happening so suddenly?"

"You don't remember, but yesterday you became a traveler with the help of Matziwa's energy body pulling your consciousness free from your head. You traveled up and down the eagles' cliffs many times without the use of your physical body, but that was only because of the presence of Matziwa. Now you must learn to travel on your own."

"But why can't I remember what happened yesterday? The last I remember, I was sitting on the ledge with you and Matziwa after nearly falling off the cliff."

"You were given a boost by Matziwa's energy to vibrate at a higher level than you are accustomed to. When and if you reach that level of vibration again, you will remember, but until then you will not. Traveling is not like your normal awareness; it's more like dreaming. But traveling takes a supreme effort to consciously initiate, control, and remember. The fire will help you to consciously vibrate at a higher level, and things will then become clearer for you. Right now, I think it's best if you go and join the jicareros and work the rest of the day with them. The physical work will be good for you. They are collecting firewood for the drum ceremony, and Jose Louis will go with you."

✦

Crazy Kieri

Jose Louis and I went to search for the group of jicareros in the mountains to the south of the village. We were walking a narrow path typical of the paths that ran all throughout the mountains like an elaborate highway system. The trail we were on was leading to a remote section of forest, but I wasn't really paying too much attention to where we were going. My mind was full of questions and concerns about all that Nichu had just told me.

Jose Louis suddenly stopped short as if he had heard or seen something alarming. Just then, someone grabbed me from behind, and I felt a large knife being held to my throat. Six other guys sprang from the bushes and surrounded us. It was the young sheriff Umberto and his gang of tewari haters.[2]

"Let him go!" shouted Jose Louis.

"Shut up, Tayau (Jose Louis's name as a jicarero)," Umberto hissed. "This doesn't involve you. You were envisioned in the dreams of the elders to be jicarero of the sun. But this tewari, what right does he have to be working with the jicareros every day, learning our ways and stealing our sacred traditions?"

"He's not stealing anything," argued Jose Louis. "You're just jealous because you haven't been chosen."

---

2 Even though many Huichol villages still happily function without roads, electricity, or running water, they still are accountable in certain ways to the Mexican government. For this reason, there exist the traditional leaders (shamans and elders) and elected officials such as sheriffs and judges. However, in my experience with Huichol villages that still live apart from Mexican society, these officials are more for show than anything else. The really important decisions are always made by the elders (kawiteros) and shamans (marakames). Umberto was one of a handful of Huichol in this village that opposed tewaris (outsiders) being allowed in the Huichol Sierra. Two of his brothers had been converted to Catholicism by tewari missionaries and subsequently disavowed their Huichol traditions, moved to Mexico City, and few years later were found murdered.

"Oh, but I *have* been chosen," Umberto cackled. "I've been chosen to teach this tewari a lesson about sticking his nose where it doesn't belong."

Umberto moved closer to me, and the big guy holding me from behind with the knife tightened the blade to my neck. Umberto put his face right up to mine, and I could smell his stale breath. "Not stealing anything, huh, tewari? What about those eagle feathers on your hat? Those feathers are sacred to my people—they're not for paleface gringos like you."

Umberto lifted his hand to grab the feathers from my hat, but at that moment Jose Louis rushed in and tackled him to the ground. Instantly, the other guys jumped onto Jose Louis and pulled him off of Umberto. Then they stood him up, and two guys held his arms. "So you want to get involved, Tayau? Okay. Now you're involved," Umberto said as he punched Jose Louis hard in the stomach, doubling him over. Another guy kicked him hard in the ribs and sent him sprawling to the ground in pain.

"No!" I shouted. "It's me you want. Leave him alone."

"Yeah, it's you I want," Umberto said as he strode back over to me. "First, I want those feathers."

I struggled to get free, but the guy holding me was too strong and the others came to help him, so it was no use. Umberto ripped the muvieri from my hat. "Hold him down!" he shouted.

They threw me hard to the ground and pinned my arms and legs. Umberto took the knife and sat on my chest with the blade to my cheek. "Let's give him a little reminder of what we do to thieves here in the Sierra, boys."

"Yeah," replied one of the others excitedly while holding my arms. "Cut him deep under the right eye, so he'll carry the scar of the thief for the rest of his life."

Whether it was anger over watching Jose Louis get beaten, the fright of being cut on the face, the aftereffect of sharing Matziwa's energy, or all of the above combined, in that moment I heard a pop at the base of my neck, and the next thing I knew, I was standing up. I felt huge and as tall as the trees around me. On the ground below me, Umberto and his gang were cowering on the ground like frightened children looking up at me. Umberto dropped the muvieri and backed away.

"That's enough!" I heard a powerful voice yell.

The jicareros were returning with the firewood, and the elder in charge of the group was standing in front of me, looking up. "Get back in your body, Jim," the elder ordered as I watched him pour water from his gourd on top of my head.

As soon as I felt the cool water, I was myself again, looking eye to eye with the elder. Jose Louis picked up my muvieri and handed it to me while the group of more than twenty jicareros with axes and machetes surrounded Umberto and his small gang. Boy, was I glad my friends had come when they did. "Come here, Umberto," the elder said gruffly.

Umberto sheepishly walked up beside the elder with his head hung low. It was obvious who was in charge. But no one noticed that he had one hand inside his *moral*, a small bag worn across the shoulders that all Huichol carried.

"Jim is a traveler now," the elder said to Umberto. "If you had any doubts before, seeing his double come out just now should be more than proof enough. The double is pure energy that is not confined to the physical body but still carries the vital essence of the being it emanates from. If we hadn't come along, his double might have seriously hurt or even killed you."

Some of the jicareros snickered as the elder looked at me with a gleam in his eye, as if he was impressed by what I had done, and he seemed to be enjoying putting Umberto in his place. Umberto looked up at the elder with hatred in his eyes. I could see his aura flashing color in a way I had never seen. Before I realized what was happening, Umberto quickly pulled his clenched fist from his *moral* and raised it in front of my face. With lightning speed, he whipped his head around to face me, opened his fist so that his palm was right in front of his mouth, and blew a strong breath into his palm, sending a cloud of powder into my face and eyes.

"You want to travel, tewari? Travel with this!" Umberto screamed as he sent the powder into my face and bolted passed the jicareros at a dead run.

I closed my eyes on reflex, but it was too late. My eyes were filled with the stinging powder, and my whole face burned as if it were on fire. I heard the elder yell, "Lay him down and give me some water!" I felt myself being pulled to the ground, and the elder began dumping water on my face. The last thing I remember hearing was "Go get Nichu—Jim is going to the land of Kieri and might not return."

I was standing on a crowded sidewalk on a busy city street. Tall skyscrapers surrounded me, blocking out the sun. The smell of a sewer drifted to my nostrils, and I covered my nose with my hand. A huge bus roared by, spewing black smoke into the air, as a million cars blew their horns.

I whirled around, trying to get my bearings, but quickly realized I had never been to this place before. The sudden contrast between having just been in the serene natural environment of the Huichol Sierra and now the smelly, polluted, and chaotic atmosphere of the city sent my head reeling, and I felt like I might pass out. The only thing on my mind was how to get out of there as quickly as possible. I didn't belong there.

With that thought, the whole scene changed, and I found myself on top of a mountain, looking down into a wide valley. I recognized it right away as the valley of Taimarita. The village was there, but it was much smaller. I could see the large round kaliway in the center and the small huts surrounding it. But most of the other huts of the village were gone—no, wait. They weren't there yet. Somehow, I was looking at the village as it was a long, long time ago.

Suddenly, I felt eyes watching me. I turned to see an enormous black wolf behind me, and I bolted down the path to escape. I ran as fast as I could, but the wolf was right behind me. Then, in front of me, another wolf appeared on the trail. This one was white. I stopped dead in my tracks and felt the black wolf jump onto my back and bite down hard on my neck. I rolled over to try and get him off me, but before I could do anything he ripped out my throat.

The black wolf, the male, moved a few paces away and sat down while the white wolf, the female, devoured me. Now I was inside of her. I could see through her eyes and hear her thoughts.

She was an incredible being, very wise, sometimes fierce but most times gentle, with an intricate knowledge of the woods and all its creatures. One day she crawled into a small cave while her mate stood guard outside. I could feel a great pressure all around me. Suddenly I was lying on the ground, looking up at the white wolf, who was licking me all over. I was her pup!

My wolf parents loved me very much, and I grew fast. I was black and white, with enormous paws that were too big for my body. Our small family traveled everywhere together, and I quickly learned the ways of the woods and how to stalk, hunt, and avoid humans. I loved my life as a wolf.

While drinking from a stream one day, I saw men approaching with guns and dogs from across the clearing where my parents were napping. The men were headed straight for them. I couldn't let them find my parents; I knew they would kill them. So I did the only thing I could. I ran out into the clearing where they could see me, and then I headed in the opposite direction, away from my parents.

The dogs chased after me, and they were fast. I could hear the men yelling behind them, but I couldn't understand their language. The dogs finally cornered me at the base of a cliff that I couldn't climb. I scrambled up as high as I could, out of the reach of the dogs—but not the guns. The men shot me as I looked over their heads behind them to see my parents, the white and black wolves, sneak away to safety after they saw there was nothing they could do for me. I had saved my parents, but it had cost me my life. The men used sharp knives and removed the skin from my body. They took my skin and left my flesh there to rot. The coyotes, vultures, and maggots made a nice meal of me.

The thatched roof of the kaliway loomed high above me, and I could see the flicker of the fire dancing in the shadows. "Welcome back," I heard a familiar voice say. I tried to sit up, but pain shot through my temples like someone had stuck an arrow in my head. "Take it slow," Jose Louis said quietly. "You've been gone for four days; we thought you might not come back. People who are attacked with Kieri usually either die or come back crazy."

I rolled to the right so that I could see Jose Louis sitting next to me. "What's Kieri?" I asked.

"Kieri is the powerful spirit that lives inside a plant with white, funnel-shaped flowers and spiny seed pods.[3] The plant grows in steep, rocky cliffs and is very rare. Evil sorcerers like Umberto's father sometimes make a powder from it to attack their enemies. It can make a person crazy or even kill."

I thought about what Jose Louis said, but thinking back to the experience I just had with the Kieri, it didn't really treat me badly, except for the splitting headache I had. I remembered what it was like to live as a wolf, and a smile crossed my face.

"What are you smiling about?" Jose Louis asked.

"I was just remembering the dreams I had. I was a wolf, and it was fantastic."

"A wolf!" exclaimed Jose Louis. "What color?"

"Well, first I was a white wolf. She ate me after her mate, the black wolf, killed me. Then I was a black-and-white wolf—their son."

"I must get my father," Jose Louis replied hurriedly. "Don't move!"

Yeah, like I was going anywhere. My head still ached tremendously, and my eyes were blurry and sore. I took a deep breath and closed my eyes. I felt safe in the kaliway; nothing bad would happen to me there.

A few minutes later, Nichu came with a few of the jicareros and a couple of elders. One of the elders I had only seen briefly once before. She was a large woman dressed in a fully embroidered Huichol dress that showed her status as an elder. As she walked into the kaliway, I thought I saw the many animals that were colorfully embroidered into her dress move as if they were alive.

"Glad to have you back," Nichu said as he knelt down beside me. "This is Marta."

The elder woman came and knelt beside me, looking into my eyes. "Jose Louis tells us you were dreaming of wolves," Marta said in a strong and melodious voice that told me right away that she was a singing shaman.

---

3 Either *Solandra* or *Datura*.

I nodded my head yes in response and then added, "But the dreams seemed more real than any I've ever had. It felt like I *was* a wolf for many weeks, and I can still remember each day and everything I did and felt."

"Marta knows more about the Kieri than anyone in the Sierra," Nichu said. "She has been watching over you the whole time you were traveling in the land of Kieri, and she has kept away the wolves."

"The vibration of Kieri is very close to the vibration of wolves," Marta said. "In the old days, the users of Kieri were called wolf shamans, as it was said that they could transform into wolves by using the power of the Kieri. Not many shamans use the Kieri anymore; it is not easy to make friends with that spirit, and it is extremely dangerous. We have all been very afraid for you; you were unconscious for four days, and suddenly this morning, shortly before you awoke, two enormous wolves, one white and one black, began circling the kaliway. There haven't been wolves in the Sierra since I was a small child—they were all killed by tewari hunters long ago. So we thought these must be spirit wolves sent by Kieri to take you away. I have been trying to fight them off all morning so they didn't kill you."

"No!" I exclaimed. "Don't hurt them."

I struggled to sit up and was surprised to see that even more people had come into the kaliway. I guess they were curious to see what was happening.

"Where are the wolves now?" I asked, excited that I might see my wolf parents again.

"They are circling the village, and the jicareros are keeping them away with sticks and rocks," Marta replied.

"Please," I said. "Let them come. They won't hurt anyone, I promise. I saved their lives, and I think they just want to say thanks."

Nichu and Marta looked at each other for a long moment, then Nichu said, "Jose Louis, tell the jicareros to leave the wolves alone."

Jose Louis ran from the kaliway. Marta and Nichu stood up and told everyone to move back and take a seat around the inside edge of the circular building. Then the two shamans placed a chair next to the fire in the center of the kaliway and helped me to get to it. They stood behind me as we faced the open doorway, waiting to see what would happen.

The wolves wasted no time. Almost immediately they appeared in the doorway, and both stared directly at me. The crowd of people sitting around the edges of the kaliway gasped in awe. Most of them had never seen a wolf, let alone two that were as big and beautiful as these.

The wolves sniffed the air, looked around for a few moments, and then walked over to me, one on each side my chair. Mother White Wolf nuzzled her wet nose on my arm while I happily ran my fingers through the hair of Father Black Wolf. I was so glad to see them, I had tears in my eyes. Mother White Wolf began licking my face as she had done when I was a pup, and immediately my headache began to disappear.

As I hugged the two wolves, wondering how in the world it was possible that they were there, I heard Marta say from behind me, "Looks like the evil deed of Umberto has turned into a blessing in disguise. Our newest traveler has acquired two powerful spirit guides!"

Into the Fire

My initiation with the fire was to start that night, and Nichu informed me that I had to collect my own firewood, enough for five days and nights. The wolves never left my side. As I walked through the village, it was easy to tell who could see them and who couldn't. The ones that could—the jicareros, shamans, and many of the adults—stared in wonder as the wolves walked alongside me. Those that couldn't—the young people not yet initiated into the tradition and the tewari traders that sometimes visited the village—didn't notice a thing as we passed.

I spent most of the day collecting firewood and stacking it inside the kaliway where I was told my initiation would take place. The wolves continued to stay close, as if they were my bodyguards. With them watching over me, I didn't give Umberto, his gang, or evil sorcerers a second thought. By the time I was finished with the wood, it was almost dark, and I was beat.

I hadn't eaten in over four days, so hurriedly I walked over to Nichu's compound, where I knew dinner would be served at nightfall.

But there was to be no dinner for me. Nichu explained that a long fast was an important part of the ritual and that an empty stomach would help to alter my state of consciousness to receive my visions with the fire. He told me to get my takwatsi, pack up all the offerings in the rirriki that the jicareros had made for me, and bring everything to the kaliway, where he would meet me shortly.

All the jicareros and elders assembled in the kaliway shortly after I arrived. The jicarero of the fire, Tataiwari, and Nichu, the fire shaman, each with two long poles, grabbed the pillow of Grandfather Fire, who was burning brightly in the center of the kaliway, and moved it clockwise from the east of the fire circle to the south. Then they fed the fire with many sticks pointing to the south. "When the fire burns once again in the east, toward the rising sun, your initiation will be complete," Nichu said mysteriously.

The first night of my fire initiation was one of the most magical times of my life. The jicareros brought their tiny violins and guitars to play the rhythm of the Huichol sacred dances. In lines of spirals, we danced around the fire, rhythmically stomping our feet to the steady beat until our movements created a spiraling universe unto itself. Our dance mirrored the spinning vortex of the our galaxy, and I felt myself as a satellite rotating around the central sun-fire. The music, dance, and energy of the people easily carried us all through the night, and before I knew it the rising sun was peeking through the doorway on the east side of the kaliway.

Soon I found myself sitting alone with Nichu next to the fire. "Your physical body must stay here with the fire for the next four days, except in an emergency should you need to relieve yourself outside. But from now on, you will not even drink water, so I doubt you will have any business of that sort to attend to."

My joyous feelings of the night quickly turned to anxiety as Nichu spoke.

"At times you will be visited by seers, shamans, and travelers. Their role is not to instruct you directly, but rather to help in setting the stage for the various phases of the initiation you will pass through. And their presence will also prevent you from sleeping, which is another important component to the ritual. But the most important thing is to simply keep the fire burning the whole time and focus as much of your energy as you can on merging with the flames. If you do that, everything else will happen quite naturally."

Nichu left, and as I put more wood on the fire, I suddenly realized how completely exhausted, hungry, and thirsty I was. A wave of anxiety hit me. How could I possibly go four more days without food or water? I looked around the empty kaliway and wondered what in the hell I was going to do for four days inside of this place. I stared at the fire, feeling very much sorry for myself as my two big, furry wolves came and lay down next to me.

The next three days and nights I spent in between feeling fully awake and partially asleep. At times, I felt like I was going out of my mind with boredom, starvation, and exhaustion, and other times I felt peaceful and content while staring into the fire. Periodically, especially at night, a shaman or elder would join me in the kaliway, but none of them ever spoke directly to me. Instead, they would simply sit with me next to the fire and chant prayers and leave offerings to Grandfather Fire.

By the evening of the third night, my wolves were getting extremely restless, and I tried to calm them while they paced back and forth around the kaliway. I brought them close to me and stroked them lovingly while sitting by the fire.

I was just about asleep when Mother White Wolf lifted her head from my lap and sniffed the air suspiciously. A strong breeze was blowing in through the door of the kaliway. I sat up straight, as the refreshing breeze had woken me up somewhat. Stiffly, I got up and fed more wood to the fire. The wind had increased even more, and I looked to see the feathers of the prayer gifts from my friends the jicareros flying on their wooden staffs. Early on the first morning of my initiation, Nichu had instructed me to place the feathered muvieris, prayer arrows, candles, gourds, and yarn drawings that the jicareros had made for me all around the inside of the kaliway. He said the intentions of the offerings would help me and maybe even serve as portals for me to travel through. I really didn't understand what he meant by that, I simply did what he suggested.

Throughout the long days and nights of my isolation in the kaliway, I was glad to have all those prayer gifts around me. They made me feel like I wasn't alone in the challenging initiation. I had made some lifelong friends in Taimarita, and I could feel that they were all behind me.

The wind continued to blow through the opening, and as I watched the feathers of the prayer gifts flying, I responded to a sudden urge and lifted my eagle-feathered muvieri from its case and raised it above my head in big circles. Goose bumps covered my body as I realized the wind blowing into the kaliway distinctly reminded me of the wind of Humphrey's property, where I first began learning how to see. It seemed like lifetimes ago since I was there, and my mind flooded with memories of Humphrey and Ronnie. A tear of emotion came to my eye as I thought of how much I missed Amy.

Staring into the fire with wet eyes, the stress of not eating, drinking, and sleeping had drawn my emotions close to the surface. I absentmindedly stroked Ronnie's feathers on my muvieri as I watched the dancing flames of the fire. The world around me slowly began to fade away as I let the flames take control of my vision and grow inside my mind.

"I've been expecting you," Humphrey said as he sat gently stroking the two wolves sitting beside him on the deck of the tree house. "I've heard you're a traveler now. I guess this proves it," he added proudly as he crossed his legs and lit his pipe.

"What am I doing here, Humphrey?"

"You're here to gain strength by remembering your connection to the wind."

As soon as he said that, many images flashed into my mind. I saw the glowing blue deer that had led me to Humphrey; Amy and me studying the correlations between quantum physics and ancient spiritual traditions at the tree house; and myself learning to read the wind and soaring through the sky with Ronnie. In an instant, a wave of gratefulness passed over me as it dawned on me how much I had learned since first coming to the tree house.

Humphrey seemed to know what I was going through, as usual, and he smiled knowingly. "Do you ever see Ronnie?" I asked him excitedly.

"Sure," he replied nonchalantly. "He's inside, waiting for you. I'm surprised he hasn't come out yet."

I turned toward the door as Humphrey said in a loud voice, "Hey, Ronnie! There's someone here to see you."

Ronnie immediately came flying out of the tree house and landed on the railing of the deck right next to me. He looked even bigger and stronger than I remembered. When he saw Mother White Wolf and Father Black Wolf, he bowed his head low, and to my delight the wolves bowed back to him.

Ronnie let me stroke his head gently for a few seconds as I gave him my full attention. I looked over to Humphrey, sitting and smoking his pipe, and strangely enough, he waved his hand as if saying goodbye. The next thing I knew, Ronnie let out an ear-piercing screech and took off.

I went with him. He flew straight up toward the sun, and in the blinding light I saw the fire and was back in the kaliway. It was now burning low, so I went to the woodpile and grabbed some sticks. When I turned back to the fire, Tataiwari and Nichu were there with their two long poles, turning the pillow clockwise toward the west.

I fed the fire with sticks pointing west. Tataiwari and Nichu each fed a stick to the fire as well and then left the kaliway without a word. I wondered at the significance of what they had just done.

With the fire burning brightly once again, and remembering how I had just traveled to the tree house, I took my necklace of rose beads off and closed my eyes. I could still see the fire in my mind's eye as I balled the necklace up in my two hands and raised it to my face. "This has to work," I thought to myself as I concentrated on the energy of the beads.

Maggie's hand felt soft but sure in my mine as we strolled through the orchard. We headed into the garden and stopped at the side of the lab. Maggie didn't say anything; she just squeezed my hand a little tighter for an instant. There wasn't really any need for words. I looked out over the grounds, and a deep feeling of love for the place and all the living beings that were part of it swept through me. With the wolves following close behind, we walked to the herb garden, and I saw my favorite rose bushes blooming. "Blood and breath," I thought to myself as Maggie squeezed my hand once more, and I bent down with closed eyes to take in a long, deep smell of a fresh rose.

I opened my eyes to the sound of falling rain. Looking out the doorway of the kaliway, I could see it was pouring outside. I longed to go out and feel the rain, but I remembered Nichu saying not to leave unless it was an emergency. Just then he walked in with Tataiwari, and the two men moved the pillow of Grandfather Fire clockwise once again, this time to point toward the north. Nichu and Tataiwari silently fed the fire with sticks pointing north and then left the kaliway.

My wolves seemed to be getting restless again, but I didn't have a clue why. Maybe they sensed something that I couldn't, or maybe this was all a dream and in reality I was still unconscious from the Kieri and they were trying to wake me up. I pinched myself on the forearm, and it stung. So much for dreaming.

Rain was coming down in sheets now, and I silently wondered how waterproof the thatched roof of the kaliway really was. Maybe I was in for a soaking. I put some more wood on the fire and sat, comfortably playing a steady beat on my drum, while looking out at the rain from over the flames. I noticed that the dry ground outside the kaliway was starting to pool and that a small puddle of water was starting to form at the open doorway. As I continued to drum, the puddle grew bigger until a small stream of water started to flow from the doorway to the center where I was sitting. I watched with great anticipation as the small stream worked its way slowly toward the fire. As the stream continued to flow toward the center of the kaliway, it grew larger and faster. "This is going to be cool," I said out loud to the wolves, who were also watching intently.

The stream of water hit the bed of hot coals from the fire, and a billowing cloud of steam rose from the ground. Immediately, I remembered the flowing lava hitting the ocean in a giant cloud of steam in Hawaii as outside a lightning bolt lit up the sky behind the cloud of steam and a tiny rainbow appeared just for an instant. And in that instant, I was gone.

I strolled through the village to the big house and found a small gathering of people ready to begin the evening meal. As I approached, a small child handed me a twig, a small gourd of water, and an unlit candle. I stood in front of the fire, placed the twig of food reverently in Grandfather's mouth, and circled the fire to stand in front of Awaul and Lauwa.

Awaul smiled at me as he dipped his flower into Lauwa's gourd and carefully touched the wet flower to my eyes, wrists, ankles, mouth, and finally to my heart while speaking in a clear voice, "May the spirit of the water bless your eyes to see clearly, your hands to make good things, your feet to walk your path with heart, your mouth to speak the truth, and your heart to beat to the rhythm of nature."

I emptied my gourd into the basin in front of Lauwa as our eyes met. In a flash, like a movie in fast-forward, I saw in her eyes the great wave that almost killed me, people laughing and joking as they happily arrived for the water ceremony, the flowing wheel of water endlessly spinning its cycles, and the multicolored water spirit emanating from the sacred spring.

Lauwa broke my gaze with a gentle movement of her head that motioned for me to continue around the circle. I bowed my head respectfully to Awaul and Lauwa, as did my wolves that were at my side, and then turned and lit my candle from the fire and proceeded around the circle and down the path to the sacred pool. Kani was waiting at the water's edge. We kissed on the cheek and held hands while facing one another in what we both felt as a very special moment. She took my candle, and the wolves and I slipped into the water.

A wet feeling in my crotch made me stand up. Looking down, I saw that I had been sitting in shallow puddle of water next to the fire, which was roaring brightly. I could barely see around me from the steam of the water mixing with the fire. As it slowly began to clear, I found myself surrounded by nearly everyone in the village.

Jose Louis handed me the clothes that I had arrived at the Sierra in. During my time with the Huichol, I mostly wore Huichol clothes because they were the most practical for the weather and the work I was doing. I thanked Jose Louis for the clothes and went behind the woodpile to change.

When I came back, Nichu told me that I should move the pillow of Grandfather Fire myself for the final time in my initiation and handed me the poles. I moved the pillow clockwise to the east position and fed the fire, sticks pointing east and out the door of the kaliway.

"You have traveled well during your initiation," Nichu said to me as the crowd went silent. "Wisely, the fire helped you travel to your places of power, to round up all of your strength and energy for the task that is ahead of you. Now you must travel to find out what your task is. It's time for you to find your purpose.

"For this, you will be sent to a place you have never been, and that will be very challenging for you. This will require much strength and intention. That's why we are all here. Joined together for a single purpose, we will help to propel you solidly down your path."

Nichu handed me a brand-new *moral* embroidered with wolves, deer, flowers, and birds. Inside the *moral* was my takwatsi, filled with all my sacred things. I slung the *moral* over my shoulder as Nichu put my eagle-feathered hat on my head in a fatherly but playful way that made the crowd chuckle.

Nichu raised his arms into the air, and everyone went silent. As he lowered them, he put one of his hands in mine and the other in Marta's, who was standing next to him. Jose Louis took my other hand, and everyone in the kaliway joined hands as Nichu began to slowly chant, "Fly, Jim, fly."

Some of the people had closed their eyes; others were staring intently at me. I looked around at all the faces that I knew and loved. "What awesome people these are," I thought to myself as I heard them all chanting slowly the three words of intention to help propel me toward my destiny. But I silently wondered why Nichu had handed me my things as if I wouldn't be coming back. I looked into the fire and immediately knew the answer, but I didn't know if I had the courage to accept it.

The chanting of my friends the jicareros, the shamans, the children, and all the other people of the village was getting stronger and louder. I knew it was time to go. I looked over to Nichu and he winked; then I looked up to the roof of the kaliway and took a deep breath. As I let my gaze fall to the doorway to the east, I focused my attention on the yarn drawing hanging above the doorway. The drawing was a nierika, a sacred portal of the Huichol to other worlds. It was the one Jose Louis had made for me, and I had placed it there at the beginning of my initiation, not really knowing why at that moment.

The firelight seemed to activate the colors of the spiral drawing, and I felt myself being pulled into its vortex. "Fly, Jim, fly" echoed through my head, and I could feel the energy and intention of the all the people fill the kaliway. In that moment, I finally understood the full purpose of the sacred building. The intention of the people was being amplified by the structure of the round and domed kaliway. The tension was so great that I felt as though I was ready to be shot out of a slingshot.

The chanting and energy of the kaliway reached its peak, and I shouted thank you to all the people as I rocketed into the nierika.

It is generally recognized that our ancestors had a wide range of medicinal plants at their disposal, and that they likewise possessed a profound understanding of plants' healing powers. In fact, up until the twentieth century, every village and rural community had a wealth of herbal folklore.
ANDREW CHEVALLIER,
ENCYCLOPEDIA OF MEDICINAL PLANTS

CHAPTER 4
Plant Medicine: Power from the Earth and Sky

Most of us "modern" people have lost the lore of our ancestors as to the preparation and usage of medicinal plants. But for shamanic cultures throughout the world where the people still live off the land, the shamans and healers, be they men or women, still retain the ancient knowledge of the medicinal value of the plants where they live, and this is one of the first things they are taught by the elders of the tribe. This was not the case for me. I didn't start to fully appreciate and learn the medicinal value of "common" plants until later in my life, and in comparison to those

117

shamans who have been working with medicinal plants their whole lives, I realize how little I really know. In terms of plants, the majority of my time on the shaman's path has been with "power plants," or those that have been in modern times classified as entheogens.

Entheogens ("creates god within"—*en-*, in, within; *theo-*, god, divine; *gen-*, creates, generates) are plants that contain psychoactive properties and are employed in a spiritual or religious context, in contrast to the same plants or other psychoactive substances used in a recreational setting. The following three stories all include experiences with sacred plant entheogens, but the first story opened my eyes to the almost incomprehensible number of medicinal plants on our planet that are not psychoactive but still have potent medicinal properties.

My inclusion of medicine experiences with entheogens is not intended to influence anyone into experimenting with them. Some entheogens can be extremely dangerous or even lethal. Please note that some shamanic cultures use entheogens and some don't. Entheogen use is certainly not a requisite experience in shamanic practice. I have included these stories simply due to the fact that for most of my life I have been in some way or another involved with entheogenic experiences and the medicine they convey.

San Pedro and Appreciation for the Medicines of Nature

One day, I was rock climbing with a friend in upstate New York and we just had made the last climb of the day—a short but difficult rock face on the side of a bigger mountain. We were walking on the top of the ridge trail when I noticed a woman with silver hair in the woods who looked like she was walking in circles and kind of walking aimlessly. She didn't seem to be in any danger, though, and I know she saw us and hadn't asked for help, so I didn't think much of it. It was a short walk to our trucks and the parking lot. I said goodbye to my friend but just as I was ready to leave, the lady in the woods popped into my mind, and for some reason I had a clear intuition to just go and see if she was truly okay.

I found her near to where I first saw her, and I struck up a conversation. She certainly was not lost; on the contrary, while talking with her, she seemed to know the area quite well. She introduced herself only as Little Fox, which is a Native American name I had heard before, and she certainly did look Native American now that I was up close to her.

While speaking with me, she noticed I had a rash of poison ivy on both my arms that was just starting to ripen, and she said, "That's a pretty good rash you got there."

"Yeah, I got it last week while getting firewood," I replied. "It's starting to itch pretty good now."

"Well, one good deed deserves another," Little Fox chuckled as she reached into a shoulder bag she was carrying. (I guess she was referring to me coming back to check on her.) "I found these little touch-me-nots[4] hiding down by the river this morning, and they are just the thing for what you've got there. I only took a few just to have around, but you're welcome to them."

She handed me some green stalks and said, "Just crush up those stems and rub the juice on your ivy, and it'll take right care of it."

I accepted the stalks, we said goodbye, and as I was walking away she said, "Hey, if you need any more of those, just come by and see me—my cabin is in the valley on the east side of Pinetop Road. Stop in anytime." I waved back politely at her, got back to my truck, and went home. That was the time I met Little Fox, and little did I know who I had just stumbled upon and the relationship that would develop between us.

The poison ivy medicine I got at the store was not working well, I so decided to try Little Fox's suggestion. But there wasn't much juice and I could only put it on one arm, and not only did I have the rash on the other arm, I also had it on my legs and even a little in my private area, which was the most annoying of all. The juice on my left arm felt very soothing and soon became the only place that didn't itch so much.

---

4 *Impatiens capensis.*

For those of you allergic to the ivy as I am and have experienced it, you know how bad it itches before it starts to heal. So after an almost sleepless night, I ate breakfast and went to see Little Fox. I had seen the cabin where she lived many times and knew right where it was. When I got there, she was sitting on her porch like she was waiting for me.

"Ah, so those little touch-me-nots did you right?" Little Fox smiled as we shook hands.

"Yeah, much better than that store-bought stuff," I replied. "I don't want to take yours or bother you, but if you could tell me what they look like and where to find them, I'll just go and get some of them myself."

I'll never forget how Little Fox's eyes lit up and the expression on her face when I said that—her expression was that of a little kid sitting by the Christmas tree, ready to rip open the first present.

"Well, okay!" Little Fox exclaimed as she clapped her hands together. "Come on, we'll go together."

She grabbed a few things from the cabin, and then we took Little Fox's pickup and drove the few short miles to the creek. "You stay here a few minutes—I'll be right back," Little Fox instructed. About ten minutes later, she returned with a bunch of whole plants, not just the stems. "Okay, here's the plant medicine for what you've got. Now, just so I know you'll be able to find them for yourself from now on, you go and find some. Take one with you to look at so you are sure you pick the right plants."

I thought it was rather strange she was going to all this trouble, but I wanted to get some more, so I headed toward the creek in the same direction that she had emerged out of the woods.

I walked up and down the creek side and all through the woods near there and could not find even one plant. Frustrated and not wanting to make Little Fox wait, I went back to the truck. She could see I had no plants and before I could say anything, she said, "Jim, it's okay; I have plenty of time. You go back out hunting. I have this wood carving I'll work on while you're gone." She reached into her truck, threw me a bottle of water, and told me to get going.

I searched for about three hours and found not one plant. I was getting hungry and discouraged and went back to the truck. "Come on, let's go back and have some lunch," Little Fox said reassuringly. When I was around her, I noticed I felt unusually calm and relaxed, so I agreed.

Little Fox made us some sandwiches, and while we sat eating somehow she steered me to the topic of my experiences with the Huichol and other indigenous people. I could tell she was completely surprised at what I was telling her, even though she did her best not to let on—especially that I had been to Wirikuta, the sacred peyote desert, on pilgrimage with the Huichol, and that I was in my second of year of a five-year apprenticeship with a Huichol shaman.

Little Fox leaned across the table toward me and asked, "Have you ever met San Pedro?"

Since I figured she was referring to a plant and not a person, I replied, "Well, I have seen it before. I have a friend in Arizona who grows all different kinds of cactus that he sells over the Internet, and I have seen it in his garden. I know it is a sacred plant, especially to the tribes in Peru."

"That's right. He's a sacred plant to many tribes in South America; that's where I met him. It seems not such a great 'coincidence,' then, that I also have a brother in Arizona who grows it. You know, Jim, he can help you in finding other plants. He has helped me many times, especially when looking for other medicine plants."

"Wish I had some," I replied as I leaned back in my chair. "Those darn touch-me-nots are eluding me."

"Lucky day!" exclaimed Little Fox as she jumped up and clapped her hands. "I happen to have some right here!"

She came back a few minutes later with a few long, tubular-shaped cactuses and put them on the table. Little Fox was very excited and with exuberance explained to me the sacred usage of the cactus and how, by ingesting a small amount, it would help me to "clear away" everything else so as to make it easier to find the plants I was looking for.

"The San Pedro grows in different forms. Some have four ribs on them, and others have five or seven or even nine. The most sacred has four, corresponding to the four directions or the four winds. That is what we have here. But it takes many hours to prepare it properly for medicine work. If you would like to meet him, come back tomorrow morning and we'll make a batch."

I was more than happy to accept her invitation. I was in a period of my life where I could honestly say I was addicted to learning about this kind of thing, and Little Fox was certainly a medicine woman. I took the plants she had collected home with me, crushed the stalks, and put the juice all over my rashes. The next day, feeling a little less itchy, I went back to see Little Fox.

Little Fox had an old-fashioned woodstove out in back of her house, and sitting on top of the stove there was a large pot. We stoked up the woodstove, filled up most of the pot with water, and added cut-up pieces of the San Pedro. We let the San Pedro cook for about six hours.

Little Fox handed me a couple cut-up stalks of the touch-me-nots and told me to take four cups of the San Pedro brew and put it into another small pot she had put on the stove. "Now, place the touch-me-nots into the small pot, and ask the San Pedro to help you find them."

We let the new mixture cook for another hour, and then Little Fox poured two small portions into cups for us to drink. "While you drink, envision the touch-me-nots," she instructed.

When we finished our cups, we hopped into her truck and headed for the creek. On the way, my vision seemed to somehow clear, and while staring out the window I became fascinated with all that I was seeing. It was like I had never been there before. Everything seemed different—more vibrant, more beautiful—like a veil had been lifted from in front of my eyes. A calm sort of euphoria spread through my body and mind.

"Go for it!" Little Fox exclaimed as we arrived at the creek. I jumped out of the truck and practically ran down to the creek. When I got there, I walked in the opposite direction of where I had previously searched and where Little Fox had found the plants she had given me.

It was an amazing experience. It was like all the plants were waving happily at me as they moved in the breeze, and I felt a sort of all-encompassing consciousness around me that all the plants and trees shared—and I also had the eerie feeling that they all knew what I was doing there.

I felt like I wanted to be closer to the water and noticed some rocks in the stream that I could step onto to get to the center of the stream. I hopped from rock to rock until I reached the center, where there was a large boulder. I knelt down on the rock and reached down and splashed my face, but I leaned forward too far and fell in. I knew the water was cold, but I didn't feel cold and the current was mild, so I just let myself drift downstream and let the water take me where it would.

After about ten minutes or so (time seemed to have no real meaning), I climbed up the stream bank and sat at the edge of the forest, looking out over the stream. I was, of course, soaking wet, but I still didn't feel cold. I saw and felt such beauty in my heart that for a while I forgot all about my mission. When I finally remembered why I was there, I thought to myself, "Okay, you little touch-me-nots—here I come!" I stood up, and all around me I saw them. You can probably imagine how surprised I was. There were at least ten plants within my view, and to my eye they each stuck out from the other plants around them like an elephant sitting on a bench in Central Park.

The first plant was growing right next to me, and as I learned from the Huichol, I asked the plant's permission before taking it and said a prayer of thanks for its precious gifts. I collected an even dozen plants in probably less than an hour since drinking the San Pedro mixture. I was truly astounded by the magic I was experiencing, and, excited to share with Little Fox, I headed back to the truck.

Arriving at the truck, Little Fox was nowhere to be found, and the truck was locked. I thought it was strange, but I wasn't worried about Little Fox; she obviously knew the woods intimately. I did, however, wonder what she was up to this time. I had met other medicine men and shamans who practiced "coyote teachings," which meant that they never really gave you a direct answer to a question but they would put you in a position to learn the answers for yourself.

I sat under a large tree near the truck and cleaned the plants with my knife. I felt happy and safe and was sure Little Fox would come back soon. But after an hour of waiting, the sun was going down, and I was starting to get cold. Another hour went by, and I started to feel concerned. I tried the truck doors again, but of course they were still locked. There was a large metal toolbox in the bed of the truck. Rummaging through it, I found some matches and within a few minutes had a small fire going. There was plenty of dry wood on the ground, and the warmth and light of the fire was all I felt I needed in that moment. It was like the circle of light created by the fire in the darkness had created my own little island, and nothing else mattered.

I'm not sure how long I sat talking with the fire (talking with the fire was something the Huichol had taught me years ago) before I looked up and saw Little Fox standing in front of me.

"I see you found the plants you were searching for," Little Fox commented nonchalantly. I looked up at her and saw the fire dancing in her eyes.

"Your first meeting with San Pedro went extremely well. You experienced with him the main powers that govern our world: the wind, water, earth, sun, and fire. And you found your plants. It doesn't get much better than that. Come on—put out your fire, say thanks to this place, and let's go home."

During the next few months, I saw Little Fox on an almost daily basis. Since I was between jobs and had some money in the bank, it was perfect timing. Whenever we got together, we would almost always go walking in the woods and she would teach me more about the plants, or sometimes she would take me to an ancient sacred site. Sometimes, on longer trips, we would stay in the woods overnight, and she taught me how to make quick and cozy shelters from downed trees, bark, pine needles, leaves, and such that would bounce the heat of the fire back onto where we were sleeping under the shelter. Being with Little Fox was like taking an advanced course on wilderness survival.

A list of the medicine plants that Little Fox taught me to how to find and use is way too long to be included here. The best lessons Little Fox taught me were the ones I used on myself, although I was also beginning to use the plants to treat my friends when they were sick or hurt. Almost always, they were surprised at how well the plant medicines worked. I developed somewhat of a reputation as a healer throughout the rock-climbing community, especially after Little Fox began teaching me how to make tinctures[5] so that I didn't have to prepare a fresh batch of medicine every time I wanted to use it. Some plant medicines could only be used when fresh, but others worked very well when used as a tincture.

One of the most amazing things about Little Fox was that the medicine seemed to follow her. Wherever we went, she could easily find whatever was needed in a particular moment or it would just be right where we were. I think this is a very clear sign of a "real" medicine person. For example, once we were out in the woods collecting plants and cleaning them, and I cut my finger with my knife. It was a deep cut, all the way to the bone, and it bled profusely. Little Fox ran off and within a few minutes came back with some mushrooms that she called "cobwebs" (*Calvatia craniiformis*). She quickly ripped off a piece of my shirt to use as a bandage, opened up one of the mushrooms, and placed the cobwebs directly into and over the cut and wrapped it. The bleeding stopped immediately. "The best thing about these little guys is you can take the rest of them home and fry 'em up in a little butter. Quite tasty!" Little Fox said in a funny sort of voice. Of course, the next plant she had me hunt for was the cobwebs.

Another time we went on an excursion for a few days and I got a bad case of diarrhea. In no time we found some heal-all (*Prunella vulgaris*). Not only did it help fix my ailment, but we added it to the salad we ate for lunch. Whenever I started to feel like I was getting a cold, especially when a runny nose was a symptom, Little Fox taught me to go down by the lake and get some sweet flag (*Acorus calamus*). The root is good for lots of things,

---

5 To make a tincture, a jar is filled with plant medicine and then pure grain alcohol is added and the medicine left to soak for 2–3 weeks. The liquid is strained, and a potent form of the medicine is poured into smaller bottles or droppers.

but if you chew on some small pieces during the course of your day, the cold or flu usually does not materialize. "But don't eat too much of it, you might start seeing things," Little Fox admonished me. (Sweet flag is also an entheogen.)

A few times, I have been helped by the "toothache" bush (*Zanthoxylum americanum*). Just find one, take off some of the bark, and chew on it to relieve the pain enough until you get to the dentist. It really works! And even though I have decades of making and working with fire, once in a while I still do get a burn. More often than not, it's from a stove rather than the fire. If this happens, Little Fox taught me to make a poultice from the inner bark of the "out of ash" (*Larix laricina*) tree. The tree gets its name for being one of the first trees to come back after a fire, so it's fascinating that it also treats burns.

About a year after first meeting Little Fox, I moved from the Northeast, spent a lot of time in Mexico, and finally settled in Arizona, so my visits and lessons with Little Fox were few and far between. She has no telephone, but my friends tell me that she still works in her garden and hunts for medicine. People bring her deer meat, firewood, and all sorts of things in exchange for her healing work and natural plant medicines and tinctures, although I would bet that even in her advanced age she could live off the land with no help if she needed to. Once in a while, I will get a package from Little Fox with some of my favorite plants from her woods that I can't hunt where I live now.

A few years ago, I arranged for her to come to Arizona and visit for a week. Boy, did we have fun! I was amazed at her knowledge of the high desert's plants and trees. Little Fox knew more than I did, and I lived there! She explained that she had visited the Four Corners region of our country often when she was younger and was taught by very wise medicine women of the area. I was sad when she boarded the plane for home, and I haven't seen her since. But she instilled in me such reverence and knowledge of the plants and trees surrounding me that I see her everywhere I look, even when I'm not in the wilderness.

One time when we went into town together, she commented that "even what your people call weeds are often medicine plants." She said this while looking out the window of my truck as we passed neighborhoods of houses with groomed lawns. With a sweep of her hand toward the lawns, I will never forget what she said. "The 'weeds' in those lawns that people kill and pull out and cut down—the plantains (*Plantago lanceolata, Plantago major, Plantago media*), the chicories (*Cichorium intybus*), the daisies (*Bellis perennis*)—they are all food and good medicine." As we passed a yard that was bathed in a sea of yellow, she swept her arm again toward the lawns and with a quick wink at me, she said with a grin, "And all those dandelions…they make a mighty fine wine."

Ayahuasca Death Lesson

The Tukano ayahuasca[6] shaman had been preparing the magical brew for days and had given me a cupful of it, which I swallowed right away. It was sunset, and the Colombian jungle felt like an unfathomable mystery of beings both seen and unseen.

Because he could read my energy field, he knew that I had experience with other powerful medicines from nature, so instead of keeping me close to him during my experience, he decided to send me into the jungle alone while the ayahuasca played out its magic.

With some trepidation, I agreed to heading off alone, without his help and experience to guide me on my "trip." At first, as I began walking, I didn't feel the intense sensations that I had heard others felt. But the stars, the jungle sounds, and the touch of the plants and trees that I brushed against all felt more alive and somehow more real or intelligent. And then everything suddenly changed. From deep inside me I felt a massive

---

6 Ayahuasca is a complex drink prepared from a powerful tropical vine (*Banisteriopsis caapi, inebrians*) and then mixed with other ingredients to achieve different strengths and experiences. Ethnobiologists note a variety of over 200 plants that are used in the different brews made by the ayahuasca shamans of South America.

churning, and I knew I would vomit. The sky, the trees, the very earth under and surrounding me vibrated in giant waves as I threw up over and over again.

When the purging finally subsided, I found myself lying on the ground and watching an incredible geometric light show whether my eyes were open or closed. It was during that time I realized that I had no body. I had left the physical realm and was traveling with purely mind and spirit. Then I saw my body lying on the jungle floor, and I knew that once again I was brushing with the ultimate fate of us all: death.

As I watched my body, I saw a sort of fast-forward version of the decomposition of my body and then the worms and vines and soil taking my body back to the earth. I experienced a spiritual reunion with the life-giving body of the earth. I was everything, and everything was me.

After a time—maybe a few minutes, maybe a few days or lifetimes—everything went black: no input or feelings at all. When I awoke, the sun was up, and I immediately hiked back to the shaman's hut. There he was, sitting on the porch as if expecting me.

He grabbed my head with both hands and examined my eyes. "You learned the lesson that death is not the end but simply another beginning," he said with a big grin.

"Because what doesn't kill you makes you stronger?" I asked.

"No, my son, what *does* kill you makes you stronger."

I was contemplating his words when he looked at me with a peculiar light in his eyes, and he asked, "You want another cup?"

I actually laughed until my belly hurt, which is the result I think the old shaman was expecting.

"No, thank you, not today," I replied.

"Okay, then—go now and live your life knowing that there may be no tomorrow…"

Mazatec Mushrooms

I went to visit a Mazatec friend in his home village in the state of Oaxaca, Mexico. My Mazatec friend, Armando, had been living and working in the urban jungle of Mexico City for the past fifteen years, but at fifty-five years old and tiring of city life, he had decided to move back to his rural village in Oaxaca to be closer to his family, the land, and the ancestral life of his people. One of the things that had always fascinated me about Armando was that during the many years we spent together while he was living in the city, he never really lost his connection to his indigenous roots. Even though he is a small man physically, he carries himself in a manner that displays his inner fortitude from his traditional upbringing, and he radiates a very powerful energy that anyone around him can feel immediately. With his dark skin, jet-black hair, pearl-white teeth, and rigid jaw line, he looks like someone who has just stepped out of a documentary about the ancient Aztec warriors, only he's wearing modern-day clothes—well, most of the time.

I arrived at the city of Oaxaca via a very scenic six-hour bus ride from Mexico City. The mountains around the city are very rugged and beautiful, and the valley of Oaxaca was one of the most fertile and thus important regions of pre-Colombian Mexico. The state of Oaxaca retains much of its pre-Colombian roots, as it has more native speakers of Mexico's indigenous languages than any other state in the country. I had never been to this particular area of Mexico, so I was very excited when Armando invited me. In planning my trip, I knew that Armando's village was about four hours from the city, but I wanted to spend a couple days in the main city that the state was named for. I found the city of Oaxaca to be very friendly, historic, and beautiful. There were people living there from all over the world, and I was more than a little surprised at the mixture of native Mexico with the cosmopolitan atmosphere that Oaxaca attracted.

After three days of visiting the city, Armando came to get me, and we drove some very rugged roads to get to the small village where he and his extended family lived. What immediately struck me was how simple their houses were but how intimately beautiful their gardens were. In this rural area, almost nothing was bought at the store. There was a central market were all kinds of products could be purchased, but most families relied on what they grew or traded with other families. Armando's family grew a wide variety of food, including corn, beans, squash, avocados, and pineapples, and they also raised turkeys and chickens. But their prized possession was definitely their coffee groves. The shade-grown Oaxacan coffee is amazingly tasty and also a sustainable product, unlike the factory-type farming of coffee that is so typical these days.

There are also many wild edibles in the Oaxacan forests and fields, including the famous psylocibe *Mexicana*, otherwise known as the magic mushroom. I knew from reading about her that the famous Mazatec curandera Maria Sabina, who used the mushrooms in her healing ceremonies, had lived in this area. She had publicly proclaimed that since the "psychedelic '60s," when thousands of "hippies" had come to her town seeking her and the "little holy ones" (her mushrooms) for degenerate purposes, they had stolen the heart of the little holy ones, who were ruined forever. I felt sorry for her. She had unwittingly given her sacred chants, her energy, and her soul for what she thought was a higher purpose, but in the end she was robbed of all those things and left only with her conscience.

That's why I was very surprised that after about two weeks of living with Armando's family and helping in the gardens and fields, I was invited to a healing ceremony where all the participants were going to ingest the magic mushrooms. When I questioned Armando about what Maria Sabina had said, he simply replied that it was her destiny to do what she had done but that did not affect the ancient traditions surrounding the usage of the sacred mushrooms, and there were still powerful curanderos who had the knowledge of the mushroom spirit.

I took what Armando said at face value, and I was actually very intrigued and excited to be invited to participate. Armando told me that one of the old grandmothers that held the most knowledge of the mushrooms would be going out the next day with one of the young virgin girls of the village to collect the mushrooms. When the mushrooms were picked by a "pure" female, they still retained all of their magic and power. The ceremony was to be held two nights from then, but before that night one of the strangest things happened to me.

After dinner, the night before the ceremony, I went for a walk down the family's quiet country lane. I walked about a mile to the center of the village, turned around, and was about halfway home when I suddenly felt a threatening presence watching me in the dark bushes beside the lane. I was all alone, so I quickened my pace just to be safe. As soon as I did that, I heard a growling noise to my left and braced myself for some kind of impact. But, surprisingly, I wasn't attacked.

I thought maybe I had just imagined the whole thing and walked over to the bushes and peered inside. There were two giant glowing eyes staring back at me! I jumped back and ran for it full-speed down the lane, toward the houses. About two hundred yards later, I heard the growling again, but this time it was to my right. I ran even faster but kept hearing the growling on either side of me, and then it sounded like it was all around me. I could see the outline of Armando's family's houses in front of me in the darkness, but just then a giant figure appeared in the road. I stopped dead in my tracks. Out of breath, I bent over and put my hands on my knees and peered into the darkness. What I saw was truly unexplainable. One second it looked like a giant black tiger pacing back and forth, the next moment it looked like a thin young woman with long black hair, wearing a colorfully embroidered long dress.

I turned to look behind me just to be sure nothing else was coming, and when I looked back up the road there was the cutest little puppy just standing there, wagging its tail, right where the tiger-woman had just been! Breathing a sigh of relief, I headed toward the puppy, but when I got about ten yards from it, I heard yelling from the small compound of houses, and one of the old grandmothers came running down the street toward me.

The puppy turned toward her, puffed up its back as if ready to fight, and then jumped into the air right as the old woman got there. The old woman yelled something in Mazatec and the puppy changed into an extra-large-looking crow and flew away into the night, yelling something at us in crow language.

I just stood there looking up in total disbelief of what I had just seen. I really didn't feel scared or freaked out or anything. Mostly I just felt a sort of numb detachment from the whole thing, and I secretly wondered if someone hadn't slipped me something in my dinner to create such vivid hallucinations.

The old lady turned away and headed back to the houses just as Armando came running up to me. He grabbed my arm and we followed the old lady into her house, which I had never been into before. The small, one-room house was curtained off into two sections, a front and a back, and I guessed the back was where she slept, because in the front part there was only a table with four chairs, a small cooking area, and a whole wall devoted to strings of different herbs and plants. The old woman, Xilonen, was definitely a curandera. I would find out later that she was the mushroom expert who had taken the virgin to the collect the little holy ones for the ceremony the next night and that she would be the leader of the ceremony.

As we entered her house, she had her back to us as she put wood on the fire of her small fireplace and told us to sit down. When she turned to us, I almost gasped, because in that moment in the semi-darkness, with the fire behind her, she looked almost identical to the young woman I had seen in the lane. But in the next moment, she looked exactly as the old woman who had chased the tiger-woman-puppy away.

Xilonen pulled up a chair, placed it right in front of mine, and sat down.

"You are very lucky she didn't steal your soul, young man," she said in a raspy voice as I looked down on her wrinkled hands weathered by years of hard physical work. I looked down simply because I felt like I didn't have the strength to look her in the eyes.

She took her right hand under my chin and raised my head to look at her face.

"You look at me when I talk to you," she said in a calm but firm voice. "In this land of the ancient people, where the sacred traditions are still maintained, there are many that come to seek and even steal power. Like that evil witch that almost trapped you tonight. She has probably been watching you secretly from the bushes for many days, and she saw your strong energy and wanted it for herself. She is a powerful sorceress from Veracruz, by the ocean, which is hundreds of miles from here. But she can travel that distance in the blink of an eye because she has mastered the art of traveling with her other body. Her magic body she can make to look like anything she wants.

"As you continue to learn and grow, there will be others seeking to steal your power. You must learn how to protect yourself in those situations. You acted like a damn fool tonight! You never run from an evil sorcerer. You make your stand or you most likely die. I am shocked that she didn't pounce on you from behind when you ran from her. Then the most stupid thing you did was fall for the puppy. She knew she could lead you right in because you love dogs and could never resist picking up a small puppy lost in the street."

Armando looked over to me with a kind of "oh well, what can I say" expression on his face as Xilonen chastised me.

"Tomorrow night," she continued, "you will come to the sacred mushroom ceremony, and you will learn about protecting yourself and be blessed by the power of the little holy ones. Go now with Armando. I doubt if that witch will be back tonight; she knows she has no power over me or Armando. And don't stray out of your hut again tonight!"

With that, Armando escorted me back to the small hut I was staying in behind his family's house. But even though it was late, I couldn't sleep—so many things were rolling around in my mind. When dawn finally came and it felt safe to come out of my hut, I could already smell the coffee brewing and eggs cooking in the house, so after stopping at the outdoor water spigot to wash my hands and face, I entered the back door of the house and was greeted by Armando's mother, who was happily cooking and singing a quiet Mazatec tune.

"I heard you had quite a night," she said in a cheery but knowing way.

"I'm not sure what to believe or not to believe about what happened," I replied as I sat down at the kitchen table.

"Believe it all," she said, looking over her shoulder at me while cooking in front of the stove.

I took a deep breath, and just then a strong wind came in through the open window to my left.

Armando's mother looked through the window and then at me. "There are many forces in this world that you have not yet encountered. Just because you don't know them doesn't mean they don't exist."

She then put a delicious plate of food down and said, "You eat now—you have a big day coming. This will be the last food you eat before the ceremony tonight. It is best to eat and sleep little before the ceremony."

Just then, Armando and his brothers walked in and sat at the table. We all ate, and I was surprised that they paid special attention to more or less joke about what happened to me the night before, although it was very apparent to me that they knew just how dangerous a situation I had actually been in.

"You ready to work with us today?" one of Armando's brothers asked. "Looks like you got little sleep."

"Yes, I'm ready. But you're right, I didn't sleep at all last night."

"That's good," Armando said. "The little holy ones will come to you much clearer tonight if you have no sleep, because your rational mind will be tired and not thinking so much. When the rational mind is slowed down, the spirit world can come through. There's nothing wrong with the rational mind—it helps us to function and do our work—but when the little holy ones are taken into your body, they like it better when all the chatter in your head is quiet. They like it quiet and peaceful in there."

"That's right," said Armando's mom, Soledad. "You boys work James hard today so he is nice and tired for tonight."

I was a little surprised to hear all this. I had figured it would be better to be fit and rested before the ceremony that I understood would last all night and that I expected would be very intense both emotionally and physically. But I had confidence in my friends, and if they thought it would be better to be sleep deprived and physically tired, I was completely willing to accept their suggestions.

Most of the day, the brothers and I cut and gathered firewood from up on the mountain and then brought it back and stacked it in the back of Xilonen's house, where the ceremony would take place, as an offering to her for leading us in the ceremony that night. It was demanding work, and by the time we were done I was exhausted, but after thanking us for our work, Xilonen made a point to tell me not to sleep or eat before the ceremony. She suggested that I just keep busy doing chores around the house or in the fields, so I gathered eggs, chopped firewood for Soledad, washed some clothes, took a shower, and finally ended up sitting on Armando's porch as the sun was setting.

When I got to the porch and sat down, I noticed that Armando and his brothers were already cleaned up as well, and they were in high spirits. A bottle of tequila was being passed around, but no one was drinking much of it. They would just take the bottle, say a prayer, take a very small swig, and pass it to the next person. I knew from not sleeping and not eating all day except for breakfast that I should do the same and just take a few small sips, even though in retrospect I remember wanting to drink more, because I was starting to feel apprehension of the upcoming ceremony. My companions, however, were totally at ease and even telling jokes and playing around with each other.

With the sun now down and the twilight receding into darkness, Soledad came onto the porch with a beautiful basket of cut flowers as her offering to Doña Xilonen and the little holy ones. With a smile but without a word, she headed off the porch, and in unison the brothers and others who were joking around on the porch got up from their seats and silently followed her. It was in that moment that I finally realized Soledad was not only a committed parent and grandparent who was almost always singing happy little tunes and was extremely good-natured and quick to laugh, she was also a highly respected woman in the community. Her name, which means "solitude" in Spanish, was more like a joke than a reality.

We arrived at Xilonen's to find there were already many people gathered in her small house. The house was dark except for a few candles placed throughout the room, and I was surprised that her hearth had no fire burning in it. The people there, most of whom I knew, seemed relaxed and happy, but the atmosphere was very subdued in comparison to other events and fiestas I had been to in the village.

Xilonen came out from behind the partition with a beautiful young Mazatec girl who I'm guessing was in her early teens. Both were wearing wonderfully embroidered dresses, and when they walked into the room, an immediate hush commenced and everyone began to find a place to sit around the periphery of the room, where colorful handwoven blankets had been set on the floor atop low wooden seats that resembled wooden pallets about ten inches in height. Xilonen sat on one of the very same pallets and the young girl stood next to her, holding a large basket of the little holy ones that were specially cleaned and blessed by Xilonen. Without any instruction, Soledad, another woman, and two men unfurled an exquisite rug in the center of the room, and in mere seconds they placed their offerings on the rug.

Right after that, everyone else got up and adorned the rug with offerings. There were flowers, fruit, bowls with coins, different types of liqueur, herbs and tree branches, unlit candles, and all sorts of other things that were hard for me to distinguish in the candlelight. Armando handed me a small stick of wood and motioned me to join him and his brothers as we added these small sticks to the other offerings as a symbol of the offering we had made earlier of providing Xilonen with a large quantity of firewood.

"Our mesa (the rug in the middle of the room holding all the offerings) is beautiful tonight," announced Xilonen. "The little holy ones will happy and grateful that you all come with such respect and gratitude."

The young girl with the mushrooms then stood in front of her, and Xilonen made many prayers over the basket and sang a beautiful song while looking at each person in turn who was sitting in a half-moon against the walls of the house. When she looked at me, the only gringo in the room, I had a sudden flashback of the night before, but it lasted only a few seconds, and when she moved her gaze to the next person, which was Armando, the flash of memory was totally gone, and I felt peaceful and very loved and fortunate to be there. I knew they did not allow many outsiders into their ceremonies.

When her song was over and she had looked into the eyes of every person in the room, Xilonen motioned to the young girl, and she began distributing the mushrooms to each person. Not surprisingly, it was Soledad who followed her with a kettle of warm tea, confirming for me Soledad's position in the community. Although it was difficult to see, it seemed to me that the young girl somehow intuitively knew how many mushrooms to give each person. Maybe she was in some way psychically connected to Xilonen, because from what I could see, she would sometimes give two or three to one person and then six or more to another.

As the young virgin mushroom-bearer got to me, it felt like the whole room got even quieter, and probably since I was the only gringo there and we had never met, she stole a glance toward Xilonen, who silently and in an almost imperceptible way nodded to her. She then placed in my palms the biggest pile I had yet seen delivered to anyone. I didn't count them in the candlelight, but I would guess there were at least a dozen mushrooms in my cupped hands.

I felt a twinge of anxiety as I ate each one and sipped my tea, and I looked up to see if the others were watching me, but they weren't. Only Soledad looked my way one time as I ate the little holy ones. I was one of the last to receive the sacrament, and it seemed that just as I was done eating my mushrooms, the young girl went around the room and blew out all the candles.

From being with the Huichol for many years during different ceremonies that always included the sacred fire, I suddenly felt extremely uncomfortable being in almost complete darkness after eating all those little holy ones. The fire has always been my ally, even in just the flame of a candle, so even though I had my Mazatec friends there, I now felt extremely alone and vulnerable.

Xilonen began to chant in Mazatec or some other language I didn't understand, but everyone else remained silent. Her solo chanting lasted about half an hour, and then one by one other people joined in. Some sang the same songs, and others sang their own. By now, it was apparent that the people were feeling the effects of the little holy ones, and I began to as well.

During the next few hours, the intensity grew, and in the pitch darkness I saw multicolored geometric designs floating around the room. I chanted the sacred songs I knew from the different cultures I had lived with throughout the years, and I also chanted in English. Drums and rattles were passed around, and I fell in love with the sound of one particular drum. I later found out that it was what is called a "talking drum," and boy did it talk to me. As soon as I started drumming on it, it became alive in my hands, and I felt like I went into a portal. I don't remember all that happened next, but I know that I saw myself outside somewhere and that for some reason I was wearing a black hooded cloak and walking all alone in the darkness.

The visions, chanting, and then dancing in the darkness went on for many hours. Some people were going to Xilonen to receive healing, and I could hear her healing chants over all the others. But sometime just before dawn, I felt like I needed to get out of there. A physical sensation came over my body that made me want to run. I think Armando sensed this and he grabbed my arm, but I was determined. I figured that if he knew I wanted to run away he wouldn't let me, so my sneaky side made a plan to just relax, make him feel I was okay, and then I would stealthily make my escape when he wasn't looking—which is exactly what I did.

I snuck out of the house and then bolted into the woods at full speed. I felt like nothing in this world could possibly catch me, and nothing did. No one followed me, and when I finally stopped I found myself alone in the woods with the first hint of morning light starting to emanate over the mountains. It was cold enough to see my breath, but I wasn't cold at all. However, I suddenly felt extremely tired, and I sat down under a large tree and rested my back against its trunk, taking deep breaths. I put my hands down on the large exposed roots of the tree and felt immediately safe.

Just then I felt another presence. Malicious. Angry. Hungry. The sound of a large animal sniffing the air and the pounding of large paws following the scent trail I had just left in the woods. Immediately, I thought of the large tiger that stalked me the night before. The feeling of safety in the arms of the large tree was comforting, but I knew that in a matter of seconds the big animal would find me.

Then the little holy ones spoke to me. Inside my head, I heard distinct voices that told me to relax, that I was the same as everything around me—I was the tree, the soil, the air. There was no separation between me and the living earth and all the beings around me. I was as big as the Mother Earth and all the living beings and all of the cosmos. My body, mind, and spirit sank deeply into the tree, and I felt a union with all of creation.

I saw the giant black cat approaching the tree, but it stopped at the base and seemed confused. It circled the tree and let out a massive roar, but for some inexplicable reason it didn't see me.

"Where are you, little one?" I heard a sweet female voice ask.

It was the witch from Veracruz come back for me, sensing that I was all alone and without protection. I could see her long black hair and dress swaying in the wind and standing right next to me under the tree. But this time she was wrong. I was protected.

"Stay where you are," the little holy ones whispered. "You are protected by us, remain with us and connected to this tree and the Earth Mother, and that evil witch will have no power over you. She is selfish and only wants your power for her own reasons. She doesn't understand the larger powers you are connected to."

Just then, I heard the witch curse, and she turned and walked rapidly away. Also just then I began to hear voices coming from Xilonen's house, and pretty soon there were people all over the woods yelling my name. They had obviously discovered that I had left the ceremony and were worried about me. But in that moment I didn't want to be found by anyone. I felt myself sink even deeper into the tree, down to the roots, up through the trunk, into the upper branches and leaves. My body was now the same as the body of the tree. I was the tree.

It was light enough now that I could clearly see the people, including my friends, looking for me. A couple of them walked right by me without any rational explanation that they couldn't see me. I was invisible. The little holy ones had cloaked me in the black cloak I had seen in my vision. Even though I felt slightly guilty at hiding from my friends, knowing they were worried about me, at the same time I had a surge of excitement in the knowledge that I was invisible from not only the evil witch but from everyone else too. It was indescribably exhilarating. I truly was the tree and the soil and the sky and the stars. My physical body was as insignificant as a grain of sand on the beach and as significant as every grain of sand, piece of soil, animal, mineral, stone, or star.

My consciousness stopped for maybe a few hours, because when I finally woke up and stood up next to the tree, the sun was already shining brightly. When I returned to Armando's house, all the people were waiting there except Xilonen, and they all gave me hugs and then some food and water, but they didn't seem overly concerned about where I had been, unlike when I had heard them and seen them searching for me earlier.

When I asked Soledad about it later, she simply said, "Xilonen saw you merging with the tree and the universe and knew you were finally protected, so she told us to leave you be. The little holy ones had taught you well how to protect yourself. You are now one with the little holy ones; they accepted you. You are welcome to stay here with us for as long as you want or return whenever you want. But, my new son, we have nothing else to teach you about these things. You are one of us now: one of everything."

Like the dream messages or the wind or whatever
belongs to the wild, the animal comes in its
own time and place … The fantastic, timeless,
spaceless happening comes when it will: not
because of you. And that is what makes it so
treasured … Curiosity in the creature, quite as
much as the human's wish to see the animal,
brings the two together.

JANE HOLLISTER WHEELWRIGHT AND
LYNDA WHEELWRIGHT SCHMIDT

CHAPTER 5

Animal Medicine:
Wise Teachers of the
More-Than-Human World

Ever since I can remember, I have felt the magic of animals, as in the above quote. Throughout my life, both wild and domestic animals have been some of my dearest and closest friends. Many of us understand the profound benefits we receive on a daily basis from a healthy relationship with our companion animals. In my case, I have been fortunate since childhood to also befriend animals in the wild, first by reading their tracks, examining their scat, and watching where they eat and sleep; then, by simply sharing the same space over time, a relationship beyond words begins to develop.

For those of you familiar with my previous books, you already know this about me. In *Ecoshamanism,* I relate some of my stories with animals, including mountain goats, bighorn sheep, vultures, rattlesnakes, woodpeckers, butterflies, spiders, flies, blue jays, deer, wild turkeys, and of course canines. Although I tend to listen and occasionally converse with animals, I have never been much of an augur (one who reads omens from animals), at least not in the way that most people do it these days.

With the rising popularity of books on animal totems, animal guides, and so on, there are lots of people who now run to a book every time they see an animal to see what it means, like people often do for finding out the meaning of dreams. In both cases, but especially with animals, my criteria has always been to examine how I feel and what lessons I have gleaned from an animal or a situation with an animal, not what someone else thinks about it. I have always felt that although specific animals can share the same sort of wisdom or knowledge in general, it is also a purely personal issue. For example, in many Native American traditions, the spotting of an owl can mean an impending death of a close friend or family member, but to me, if someone from the city is out in nature and has never seen an owl before spots one, it could simply be a gift or an acknowledgment of higher awareness, because owls are usually very difficult to spot. Sometimes a chicken crossing the road is just a chicken crossing the road.

When you have a genuinely numinous experience with an animal, you will feel it for sure, and it won't be necessary to run off and look it up in a book. The three stories I've included here are of animals that most people never see in the wild, and they dramatically reveal the interconnection of all life. But I haven't included them because they are so much more special than any other; rather, they are unique in the fact that their medicine rarely gets to be shared with modern people.

Condor

Today, the majestic California condor (the only condor in North America) is one of the rarest birds in the world. But in Pleistocene times, thousands of condors ranged from Canada to Mexico, across the southern United States to Florida, and north on the East Coast to New York. By all accounts, the arrival of Europeans to North America and the subsequent colonization and modernization of the United States rendered the condor to near extinction. Shooting, egg collecting, loss of habitat, and eventually poisoning from cyanide traps meant for coyotes, lead bullets left in the remains of animals killed by hunters, and power lines traversing their habitat ultimately led to only twenty-two condors alive in the United States by 1982, and only in California. In 1987, a controversial decision was made to capture and bring in the nine remaining condors left in the wild, and so the only chance left for saving the condor was the captive breeding program that was put into place by various institutions, led by the San Diego Wild Animal Park and the Los Angeles Zoo. Throughout the years, the California condor conservation project has become the most expensive species conservation initiative in U.S. history, totaling over 35 million dollars so far. Although still an endangered species, the conservation efforts have produced dramatic results, especially for a species that typically lays only one egg every year or two and doesn't even start reproducing until around six years of age.

Happily, there are currently around 350 live condors in North America, 170 in captivity and 180 flying free in California, Arizona, and Utah, as well as Baja, Mexico. My first experiences with the condors happened in the Grand Canyon and later in areas of southwest Utah around and in Zion National Park. The release of condors in the Grand Canyon and the sheer cliffs that the condors like to nest in encouraged the condors to reinhabit one of their ancestral homelands. However, I have seen and been with more condors in southwest Utah in recent years primarily, I think, because there is simply more food there. Between large sheep herds and more deer, elk, and cattle, the carcasses of dead animals that the condors feed on are much more plentiful, and the condors like the higher elevation, especially in the heat of the summer, and the carcasses left by hunters during hunting season.

Although I have done some historical research on the condor and conservation efforts, my knowledge of this huge bird comes primarily from experience. They are so large (a nine-foot wingspan is typical) that while looking for them I have often confused them with distant planes flying high and far off in the sky. This situation led me to buy a high-quality spotting scope so I could clearly see the birds and other wildlife, even from far away. The areas where condors live have such vast open spaces that first spotting them with a scope is much easier than coming upon them by chance. Plus, they are very shy of humans, for good reason, and the captive breeding programs use hand puppets of condor's heads to feed the young condors so they don't see their human keepers and thus don't imprint on humans as being a source of food. While visiting the Grand Canyon, which is only two hours from where I was living at the time, I had seen many condors flying and roosting, but once I had my scope I was more easily able to view the intimacies of the condors' behavior in the wild.

My first really good experience with the scope happened as I was hiking near the Virgin River in northern Arizona. Looking down into a long meadow, I noticed what appeared to be coyotes feeding on something and there where a few birds circling around the area. But after getting my scope out, I saw that they were not coyotes at all—they were condors. I had forgotten how huge these birds are; their bodies can be four to five feet long. It appeared that the two condors had the carcass of a mule deer all to themselves, which was not surprising, as they have few natural enemies and will fight off most other birds and sometimes even four-legged carnivores. The birds flying above them were mostly turkey vultures and a golden eagle, all waiting their turn.

Now that I knew where they were and that they were feeding on the ground, I couldn't resist getting a closer view of the condors without disturbing them, so I stealthily meandered down the slope and through the cottonwood, elder, and ash trees. Coming through the trees I had lost sight of the condors, and by the time I got to the edge of the meadow, they had flown away. Still curious, I walked another quarter mile and found the carcass. It indeed was the carcass of a very large mule deer.

But upon seeing it, my stomach turned as I realized that its antlers had been cut off. That could only mean one thing: hunters with no respect for the animal they had killed. And worse yet, since the hunters hadn't taken the animal (the usual and lawful practice is to tag the deer, remove the guts, and take the deer for processing of the meat), they probably hadn't taken the meat either (or maybe just a few of the choicest cuts). This meant that the lead bullet(s) was probably left in the carcass of the deer—a bad situation, because the biggest current threat to the condor is lead poisoning from eating bullets left in carcasses. Throughout the years of the condor conservation program, many birds released into the wild have died from lead poisoning. Unfortunately, condors will eat just about anything. In California, a chick born from released parents looked sickly; upon examination during surgery at the Los Angeles Zoo, doctors found that it had ingested four bottle caps and a screw top, three electrical fittings, five washers, thirteen .22-caliber shell casings, one .38-caliber shell casing, a shotgun shell, several pieces of plastic bags, about a quarter cup of broken glass and a similar amount of broken plastic, a few small pieces of fabric, four small stones, a metal bracket, a piece of wire, and a few small pieces of rubber.

Examining the mule deer carcass thoroughly, I couldn't find where the deer had been shot. So much for removing the bullet(s)—I was just praying that the condors hadn't eaten any lead because this was the perfect scenario. There was enough left of the carcass that there was a good chance they would be back, so I moved back to the edge of the woods and set up my small portable blind (this is basically a small, tentlike enclosure that is camouflaged and has specially designed mesh windows so that you can see out but it's difficult for animals to see in; they are especially useful for condor watching, as the condor has a very poor sense of smell). The condors didn't return that day, and during the night I heard some animals in the area, probably coyotes. At first light I spotted the coyotes and scared them off the carcass, knowing the condors probably wouldn't land with them there.

Just before 10 AM the condors came. I was so excited I was barely able to keep still in my blind. With my scope and binoculars I could see the condors perfectly—my first time truly up close with free-flying condors. They tore into the carcass and gorged themselves. Like most other carnivores, condors will eat all they can when they get the chance. But after a short while, a group of five more condors came, and there was a lot of shuffling and hissing around the carcass as the vultures sorted out the hierarchy. My two birds fared well and kept feeding until apparently full. With my scope, I could see that all seven birds were tagged on the wings, and I wrote the numbers down in case I would ever see them again. Finally, cold, tired, and hungry, but supremely happy, I waited for all the condors to leave, and then I packed up and headed for home.

Many years before I became interested in condor watching, I went with a friend for my first introduction to technical rock climbing. I still remember my friend's words well: "I'm happy to introduce you to this sport, Jim, but don't hold me responsible for what happens next." What she was referring to was rock-climbing addiction, a condition that happens very easily once one gets started and feels the thrill that is like no other—which is exactly what happened to me. Now I had found another sort of addiction that was almost as powerful—condor watching—and for the next few years, I went on numerous excursions into the wilderness to view these rare, magnificent creatures.

Hunting season is like a smorgasbord for condors, and it is one of the easiest times to see them. During the big-game seasons that typically run from August to December, fresh gut piles from successfully killed big game such as deer, antelope, elk, javelina, bighorn sheep, bear, and even buffalo are left behind by hunters, and many animals that have been wounded but not immediately killed often die from their injuries but are never found by their hunters. For the condor, the safest hunting season is the archery season in August and September, as the archery arrows contain no lead, unlike the bullets used by rifle hunters. Thankfully, in California lead ammunition was banned in 2007 for the hunting of big game in condor habitats. The Arizona Fish and Game Department has also been very proactive, and Utah is working toward legislation as well. In Arizona, the distribution of information given to hunters about the hazards of lead ammunition in condor country was such a success that by 2008, more than 80 percent of hunters switched to copper bullets, with 93 percent of those reporting the copper bullets were equal to or better in performance than lead bullets. Whether you are for or against hunting, this gesture of responsible action by Arizona hunters and the California ban on lead in condor areas will save the lives of hundreds of condors and shows the condor the respect it so rightly deserves.

My love and respect for the condor blossomed throughout the years of observing them, and I gradually learned that they are highly social creatures, with etiquette and rules within their communities, and that they love to play, especially the young ones. And even though they eat carrion that would make many other animals sick, they are extremely clean and are constantly preening themselves. It's common to see a condor sit atop a tree and preen continually for over an hour. The bald head and neck of the adults is a physical adaptation to keep them clean as well, but before they lose their neck hair, the young and juvenile condors are super cute and fuzzy looking. The juvenile's furry, ashen-colored head and black body, wings, and beak make it one of the most striking birds I have ever seen. One juvenile in particular, along with its parents, stole my heart forever.

I was rock climbing in the Virgin River Gorge with a friend one day during the beginning of archery season, so I had brought my scope with me in case I saw some condors flying or feeding. About halfway up the cliff face, I saw something shoot over the sky above me but had no idea what it was. Continuing to climb, I found a nice ledge to make an anchor, and my partner began to climb up behind me. As soon as he started to climb, a giant condor came over my head and in one graceful sweep made a 180-degree turn, headed right for the cliff face about a 100 feet to my right, and disappeared into the cliff! I wanted to keep watching but I had to pay full attention to pulling the rope slack for my partner as he climbed. After he reached me, we both sat comfortably on the ledge, and while getting my scope from my pack, I told him what I just seen.

A few minutes later another condor appeared; a magnificent adult bird, she (I'm guessing it was female because it looked slightly smaller than the first one) was sitting on a ledge above and to the right of where we were. With my scope I could see her perfectly, and to my great delight I finally got to see something many people don't know about condors but that condor enthusiasts go gaga over: looking out over the beautiful scenery of the forest and gorge below her, her head changed colors! At first her bald head and neck were a dull reddish color with a grayish area on her neck and hints of yellow, pink, and orange. But just before she took off from the ledge, her whole head and neck flushed a pinkish red, and a few moments later she jumped into the sky and soared toward the gorge. Sweeping back and catching a thermal draft, she flew in large circles, climbing higher and higher, until she finally flew out of view behind the cliffs above us. I was ecstatic, for this was the first time I had viewed a "switching" close up, and by witnessing the switch of the parents, I knew there must be either an egg inside the cliff or a young condor still not able to fly.

Condors are monogamous once they find a mate, and they share responsibility for raising their young, so they constantly take turns (switching) with the egg or youngster until it can fly. Sometimes the mom or dad will be gone multiple days or until it finds food to bring back and regurgitate for the baby. Needless to say, I went many times to see what was happening with the small family, but not wanting to disturb them, I didn't climb in the area again. There was fairly dense brush and woods below the cliff, and now that I knew where the little cavelike opening in the cliff was that they were using for the nest, I had a better view from the ground and inside my blind. A few weeks later, I was rewarded for my patience of waiting for days on end without seeing the adult condors hardly at all.

All of a sudden, a very young condor—I'm going to call it a "he" just because I had the feeling it was a boy—came clumsily walking out of the cave and onto the ledge that ran horizontally in front of the cave. He was a fuzzy, dark color and his feet looked way too big for his body, as did his beak. He was a condor, all right, but in this stage he looked like a funny caricature of his parents. I was elated to finally know that the parents had successfully hatched a wild egg and that I was probably the first person to ever see this new member of the condor community.

Throughout the next two months, I watched the baby when it would appear; about the size of a duck, he grew into true condor form and a little more than half his parents' size. Even though I don't believe that they even knew I was there, a special bond with these birds developed inside me. I knew I couldn't or shouldn't help them, except keeping them from human encroachment, but somewhere deep inside me, I felt responsible for them. They had given me such remarkable gifts—especially the youngster as he played around, stumbled on his awkward feet, and waited patiently for days at a time for one of his parents to come back with food.

Another month later, I set up my blind in my usual spot, but after two excruciating days of waiting, the condors did not appear at the cave or the ledge. I was heartbroken. It felt equally or even more painful than breakups I've had with women in my life! The condor family was gone, and I had no idea where they went or if I'd ever see them again. I decided right then that I wanted to climb up to the cave, but I couldn't that day—the climb was way too difficult and dangerous without gear and a partner.

I went back a few weeks later with a friend, and we climbed to the cave but there was nothing except a few remnants of downy feathers and lots of dried poop. With a tear in my eye, I turned and looked out. Amazingly, I suddenly felt that my vision was considerably more acute and that I was seeing through the amazing eyes of a condor. As I looked up the canyon, I noticed a group of birds flying in circles about a mile away. Quickly I grabbed my scope and gasped at what I saw. A large group of condors were circling, and within that group I spotted at least three different smaller, younger condors. I just knew that "my" family was among them, which meant that my baby was now flying! I regretted not seeing his first clumsy flights out of the cave and into the trees, but knowing he was flying with his family and larger community was an awesome feeling, and I left that day with an inner glow that I have rarely experienced.

I returned the next month and ran into an elderly gentleman as I was hiking up the canyon. His name was Chris, and I immediately got the feeling he was not a newcomer to being out in the wilderness. Chris had neatly trimmed, long silver hair and looked to be at least part Native American. While speaking with Chris, I noticed that aside from his backpack he had a spotting scope in a case slung over his shoulder, and I asked him about it. He began to tell me about spotting condors, and we ended up walking together up the canyon. Seeing that I was more than interested, Chris shared with me some amazing condor stories. It turns out that he had spent many years volunteering with condor conservation efforts in California, and although not in official service anymore, he still retained a passion for condors and loved to see new birds. I told him about my abandoned condor nest and with a knowing glance he simply said, "Let's go have a look."

When we arrived at my old spot where I used to set up my blind, we scoped out the cave site high above us, but there were no condors. We sat down and both ate a little bit of the food that we had each brought with us. Engrossed in eating and conversation, all of a sudden shadows fell over us. Looking up, we saw three condors flying; within seconds, they were perched on the ledge in front of the cave entrance. It took all my effort not to jump up with joy. Instead, both Chris and I instinctively and very slowly got out our scopes.

After a few minutes of watching them preen and jump around, paying close attention to the smaller one, Chris turned to me with a smile and said, "They almost always come back to the nesting site, especially during the first year or so." I was so excited to see them again that my hands were actually shaking. This was the first time I had seen them up close since before the baby could fly. We spent the next few hours watching them, and the young one seemed especially playful and inquisitive. Chris explained to me that through many years of research, condors have been found to be so highly social and have such distinct personalities that scientists now often compare their behavior and intelligence to that of primates.

With only a few hours of daylight left and a long walk back, we said goodbye to the condors and headed out of the canyon. After just a short while, Chris stopped and examined the ground and then studied the trees above us. "There's condor poop here and many small broken branches in the trees above us," he stated. "I'd be willing to bet that this was one of the places that your young condor first flew to after leaving the cliff and where he began to learn to fly. Undoubtedly, while he was learning, his parents kept a close eye on him and made sure he roosted high above the ground in these trees at night to avoid predators on the ground. They probably all roosted in this area for many days or weeks until the youngster could fly properly. If you look around, you may find a present."

Chris was right. Without looking long, I found an enormous black and white condor feather, and my heart jumped. But then I remembered that it was illegal to possess them under federal law, and my heart sank. I looked at Chris, and he seemed to know what I was thinking. "I won't tell if you don't," he said solemnly. "Those condors are a part of you now and have a special place in your heart. You deserve that feather, young man; keep it safe and in a special place. Use it only when you pray, just like we do in my tribe (the Yuroks in California). The condor flies the highest of any bird we know, and so it is the one we ask to send our prayers to the upper worlds and the heavens. Knowing these condors in the wild has put you closer to the creator. For that, you should feel honored."

Horned Lizard

The horned lizard is a very remarkable creature. Often referred to as the horned toad or horny toad because of its rounded body and blunt snout that resembles a toad, it is neither a toad nor a frog but part of the Phrynosomatidae lizard family. I had never met a horned lizard until the time I was spending a month or so living with my Wirrarika friends in the western Sierra Madres in Mexico.

During my first few years with the Wirrarika, except for mealtimes and during ceremonies, almost all my time was spent with the men and boys of the tribe. Wirrarika women are very shy toward outsiders and especially gringos, but slowly they began to trust and accept me more and more, especially the female elders and shamans, which was great for me as they hold so much knowledge and the powerful energy of the feminine. This story is about what I learned one magical day from the Wirrarika women and the horned lizard.

In the Wirrarika tradition, the art of weaving and the mastering of the art is held in the most high esteem and is almost exclusively done by women. Nowadays, most Wirrarika women trade for or buy commercially made wool or cotton thread for the weavings they make into bags and bag straps, large and small belts, ceremonial items, and sometimes clothing. The commercial wool and cotton thread is not only easier to obtain and process but it also comes in hundreds of brilliant colors and enables the weavers to weave the multicolored patterns and symbols they see while ingesting the peyote cactus during ceremonies. It is these patterns, as well as the patterns they see in nature, that give Wirrarika woven items their power and magic. The designs are often so intricate and unique that it is not uncommon for Wirrarika living in a village far away to recognize another Wirrarika master weaver by the designs she has weaved.

In the past, Wirrarika weavers used a wide variety of natural fibers for their weaving, which included animal, plant, tree, leaf, seed, sheep's wool, and cotton. The dyes used in coloring were extracted from plant and tree sources, which was very time consuming and labor intensive. Much of the art of using natural plant dyes is being lost by the availability of commercially produced fiber, but there are still some Wirrarika women and shamans who retain this knowledge and will use the natural plant dyes for small woven ceremonial items and offerings left at sacred sites. The hunt for a specific plant to be used as a natural dye is what led me to my experience with the horned lizard.

Fernanda (I'm using Spanish, not Wirrarika, names for the story) was about nine years old and already an accomplished weaver under the tutelage of Augustina, one of the village master weavers and a shaman. One day, as a guest of Augustina, I was sitting watching a small group of women weaving, and a man suddenly appeared whom I did not know. All the women stopped weaving and seemed to be discussing something very important with the man. What I found out was that an important elder had died, and the man was requesting that Augustina make a small woven piece that would wrap a tiny crystal holding the power of the elder, which would be placed to live in the family temple. I had heard of this tradition before but of course wanted to learn more. Augustina decided she wanted to weave a traditional piece with traditional dyes and asked Fernanda to go and find some wild indigo (*Indigofera suffruticosa*) for making a blue dye. Extremely curious, I asked Augustina and Fernanda if I could go along on the hunt, and they both agreed, so off we went.

Fernanda was a sweet, animated, playful, and intelligent Wirrarika girl, and since I had Augustina's blessing to go with her, that seemed to put her totally at ease with me, and we had a fun time roaming the hills in search of the wild indigo. A few hours into our search, we passed a large boulder, and Fernanda stopped dead in her tracks. Silently, she pointed toward the top of the rock, and there I saw the horned lizard. Fernanda whispered to me that she wanted to catch it and instructed me to carefully, and with as little noise as possible, go around to the other side of the big boulder and then slowly climb up it so as to not scare the lizard but simply have it move down the rock on her side, where she would be hiding to snatch it up. The plan worked perfectly except when Fernanda went to grab it, somehow her arm went right through the rock and was stuck.

I couldn't believe what I was seeing. Fernanda's arm was inside the rock up to her elbow. She looked at me with a horrified glance and tried with all her might to get her arm free. Then I joined in, but I pulled on her body so hard I thought I would injure her, so I stopped. Not knowing what else to do, I told Fernanda I was going for help and took off as fast as I could run back to the village. I found Augustina and told her what had happened. I was frantic and out of breath, but she took the news in stride and calmly asked me to take her to Fernanda.

When we arrived, Fernanda was crying and shaking with fear. I couldn't blame her one bit. I was completely freaked out myself and still couldn't believe what I was seeing. Augustina calmly explained to Fernanda that the horned lizard was very tricky and demanded respect but was a worthy ally if one could complete a five-year apprenticeship with it. I suspected Fernanda already knew this and that's why she wanted to catch it. The magical horned lizard is an ally to master weavers, just as snakes and certain other reptiles are. Augustina asked Fernanda if she wanted to complete an apprenticeship with the lizard to become a more skilled weaver, and the young girl nodded her head yes as she wiped away tears with her free hand. Augustina then told Fernanda to speak clearly and respectfully to the lizard that was still in her hand and embedded in the rock. She was to tell the lizard why she tried to capture it, to ask permission to take it back to the village, and to promise to take care of it and provide plenty of ants, which was its favorite food. Fernanda did as Augustina said, and with that her arm was let free, and there sat the lizard, with a satisfied look on his face, in her palm.

Augustina told Fernanda to go find Antonio, her husband and a well-respected shaman, and ask him to help make her make a home for the lizard while she collected the wild indigo that she felt sure was very near because of the presence of the lizard and what had just happened. I went back to the village with Fernanda, we found Antonio, and together we quickly built a small enclosure in the back of Fernanda's family hut. The enclosure had a small opening and Fernanda was afraid the lizard would get away, but the shaman explained that if she kept her promise to the lizard, he would come and go and be there when she needed him. That was her test. If she didn't take good care of the lizard, it would leave for good, and she would be punished by the magical spirit of the lizard.

Later that day, the unbelievable happened again. Augustina told Fernanda to go throughout the village and spread word that all the women and children should come to her house for a special blessing. She also asked me to come.

When everyone was assembled, Augustina took the lizard and, saying a few words to it, held it up and squeezed it really hard. I had not a clue why she was squeezing the lizard like that. I guessed something special was supposed to happen, but nothing did. Then, with a smirk, Augustina placed the lizard on the ground and put a small gourd bowl on the ground directly in front of it. She grabbed the lizard by the horns and twisted, and lo and behold, blood squirted out from the lizard's eyes, right into the gourd. I thought maybe she had intentionally or unintentionally killed it, but she pulled the horns again and blood squirted from its eyes once more. Augustina then took out her knife and cut a small section of the lizard's tail off and collected more blood in the gourd. With that done, she gave the lizard back to Fernanda, and with her feathered shaman's wand she began to bless the women and children with the lizard's magical blood. Fernanda went first, and I second. She placed a tiny bit of blood right above each eye and on the inside of each of our wrists.

While Augustina was blessing the rest of the people, I took Fernanda aside and asked her why Augustina needed to harm the lizard for the blessing. "Oh, she didn't harm him," she replied. "The horned lizard naturally squirts blood from his eyes when needed, and his tail will grow back just like all lizards' tails do. Don't worry about him—he's happy he could help us, he just told me so—but now he is hungry, and I'm going to find him some ants."

Whether it was simply the power of suggestion or really the spirit of the horned lizard, from then on Fernanda's weavings took on a whole new dimension and quality that was truly amazing to see. The shaman Augustina didn't seem surprised at all. As for me, after the blessing with the horned lizard, it suddenly seemed that I could understand the Wirrarika language much better, and I had a much easier time finding plants when I would go searching for them.

———————◆·◆———————

Cougar

I met Kyle, a striking Navajo man in his thirties, when I was hiking one day with my canine companion, Sophie. "Does your German shepherd hunt animals for you?" Kyle asked while petting Sophie's head. "Nah," I replied.

"She likes to chase, especially deer and sometimes rabbits or javelina, but if she catches up to them, she doesn't harm them. She lives a happy life and has no desire to really hunt or kill anything. She also has been trained as a search and rescue dog, so she loves all people—the kids around where I live play with her all the time. She's a good dog."

"Wish I had a nose like this," Kyle said while stroking Sophie's long snout. "If I had a nose like this, I would smell everything so much better. I once saw a dog find a man buried in an avalanche of snow eight feet deep. That was incredible how the dog found him with his nose and saved the man's life. I've read that they are even training them to smell diseases in us humans. These dogs seem to be as useful as our medicine people. I can't have one, though—at least not yet; I still love to travel too much, and I can't take a dog with me everywhere I go. Wouldn't be fair for the dog. Maybe someday when I settle down."

While Kyle had the Navajo accent in his English speech, he was wearing traditional Navajo clothing, not jeans and cowboy boots unlike most Navajo I know. And he was definitely well educated. I guessed he had a university degree but also that he had been taught the traditions of his people and had embraced them and integrated them into his life in the modern world. As it turns out, I was correct on both counts.

Kyle and I became friends that day, and we exchanged cell phone numbers and got together for hikes and excursions whenever our schedules allowed. I showed Kyle some of my favorite places that he didn't know about, and vice versa. Many times I would bring Sophie, but I'd have to leave her home when we visited places where we had to climb steep cliffs that Sophie couldn't climb. Kyle and I were both in excellent physical condition, we were both avid rock climbers, and we made a good team.

One day while walking in a deep canyon with dense brush growing up on either side, Kyle stopped suddenly. "It rained here last night, and look at this—there is a big cat around here somewhere," he said to me as he bent down to examine the track, his long, jet-black hair blowing in the breeze. I tried not to laugh at how much he looked like he had just stepped out of a history book or could have been a character right out of *Dances with*

Wolves or some other movie. But Kyle was no Hollywood character, he was the real deal, and I had come to realize he was an expert tracker. He could tell so much about a single animal or human track that he blew my mind on several occasions. He might not have Sophie's nose, but I sure wouldn't want him tracking me down if I was a fugitive in the wilderness, for he surely would catch me. Kyle taught me a lot about tracking, and after a few months I was getting pretty good at finding and analyzing the tracks of both animals and humans. As my skill increased, the tracking of deer, javelina, and humans became second nature, and I was beginning to get quite good at smaller game such as coyotes and rabbits. Kyle was an excellent teacher, but one day he saw how confident I was getting. "Hey, Jim," he said with a knowing smirk, "I have been seeing more cougar tracks down in the canyon by the creek lately, near to where we first met. If you want a real challenge, to prove you are a tracker, then take a picture of one for me."

I accepted Kyle's challenge but asked about the reason for the picture, and he explained, "There are only two things that can kill a cougar in these parts: loss of their home range by developers, and hunters with hound dogs and rifles. These cowardly men that hunt cougars with dogs are the laziest hunters the world has ever seen. Most times now they put radio collars on the hound dogs and watch on the GPS to see where the dogs are, and when the dogs stop in one place, then they go find the dogs that cornered the cougar and shoot it from ten feet away. My father told me he even knows some guys who have lots of money and they pay these other guys with the dogs to get a cougar up a tree, and then these guys with the cougar call the rich guys on the phone and tell them where they're at, and then the rich guys go and kill the cougar. The worst part is that unlike a real hunter, they don't even eat the meat. They usually take the hide and the head and leave the rest. It's so sad. Here in Arizona, hunters kill between 250 and 350 big cats a year just for the sport and nothing else. Most have little respect for those amazing creatures. Without the hound dogs, rarely would a modern-day hunter ever be able to kill a cougar; they simply lack the skills necessary. If you are able to stalk one and get a good picture, then you have made the next step in being one with your surroundings, for to get close enough to a cougar in the wild to take its picture, you must be in tune with the land and the wind and be skilled in both mind and body."

With much practice and patience, I was able to stalk and sneak up on many animals, including black bear, but as Kyle said, the cougar was elusive and the greatest test. About my second week of trying, I actually followed one for a whole day, catching brief glimpses, but upon walking back home defeated and with no picture, I saw that the cougar had actually been stalking *me*—over the top of my tracks were the cougar's tracks! Kyle said that the cougar had probably seen me lots of times during those weeks and was curious about me and what I was doing and wanted to check me out closer, so it followed me and was playing games with me.

I spent a whole year, a couple days almost every week, stalking the elusive cats, until one day I was sitting quietly, resting my body against a large sycamore at the edge of a clearing. Looking through my binoculars, I spotted a large cougar crouching in the brush on the other side of the clearing, watching me from about fifty yards away. Excited and nervous, I slowly reached for my camera. Just then, the big male cat stood up, walked a few feet into the clearing, and nonchalantly stretched out each of his back legs before he sat down facing me and yawned just before he crept back into the brush and disappeared like a phantom. Ironically, after all the hard work, the cuts and scratches scrambling through the brush and climbing trees, and the hundreds of hours of tracking, my precious photo of the cougar was of him yawning at me. If that isn't a lesson in humility, then I don't know what is.

Kyle laughed his guts out when I showed him my photo. I couldn't help but laugh with him. When we finally stopped laughing about it, he became more serious and actually congratulated me. "After so much time and effort of blending in with trees, plants, and other animals of the forest, and by having respect and doing no harm, that cougar gradually accepted you as simply part of his environment and felt comfortable with you being there. That is quite an accomplishment. You may never see him again, but for that one moment in time you were just another creature of the forest to him, and the oneness you have achieved with the land will always be a part of you now."

As Kyle spoke those words, I realized that his challenge to me was never really about the photo of the cougar at all.

Sacred sites have the power to heal the body,
enlighten the mind, increase creativity,
develop psychic abilities, and awaken the
soul to a knowing of its true purpose in life ...
Ancient legends and modern-day reports tell
of extraordinary things that have happened
to people while visiting these places.
    MARTIN GRAY

CHAPTER 6

Medicine of Ancient Sacred Sites: Knowledge of the Ancestors

Sacred sites such as Sedona, Mesa Verde, the Hopi Mesas, Uxmal, Tulum, Tula, Teotihuacan, La Venta, Machu Picchu, Avebury, Stonehenge, Lourdes, the Parthenon, Dome of the Rock, and Mecca have been a fascination of mine since I was a young child. Throughout the years, I began to use the term "power spots" when describing them simply because many sacred sites would still contain unusual power, even if humans weren't around to consider them sacred. Plus, many of my personal power spots in wilderness areas do not have any sacred buildings or ruins associated with them. These places exude power from the natural world as well as the underworld. The following three stories include sacred sites, power spots, and visiting entities from the spirit-underworld.

The Guardians

The majestic red rock formations of Sedona, Arizona, are awe inspiring and truly powerful in their potential to affect human consciousness. For millennia, the Sedona area has been considered a sacred place, and to this day people come from around the world to steep themselves in the unique energy that resides here. Sedona is where I live, work, and play. I, along with thousands of others who live here, have found a deep connection to this area that words cannot adequately describe. This connection inspires creativity and freedom of thought, but paradoxically, at least for me, the towering red rock mountains are not so much comforting as they are ominous. Here, the beauty and magnificence of the red rocks meet the harsh reality of the desert chaparral, a landscape at once seductive but also potentially lethal if you were to get lost or run out of water.

Sedona lies within the Coconino National Forest, and as a highly experienced guide I am permitted, through the Forest Service, to take people into the red rock wilderness as a commercial activity. So I'm not too worried about getting lost or running out of water, but there are plenty of other forces at work here that one must be respectful of. This is a story of one of the many forces I have encountered here.

Since my teens, I have been almost obsessed with visiting and discovering ancient sacred sites that include ruins, petroglyphs, and pictographs. My fascination only grew when I moved to Sedona many years ago and began visiting the ancient sacred sites of the people the archeologists call the Anasazi. Over the years, I have visited and discovered over fifty ancient sites, but I am always looking for the most secret ones that I haven't yet found.

One day, I was casually driving on a very remote, bumpy, and rock-strewn dirt road in the Secret Mountain Wilderness Area just outside of Sedona and noticed there was a canyon off to my right that I hadn't yet explored. I stopped the truck, and, while looking into the canyon, my trusty sidekick Sophie (a female German shepherd) started whining and spinning circles in the back of the truck. Sophie is definitely a shaman in a dog's body, so I knew we had to check it out.

I found a place to park the vehicle, and Sophie and I headed into the canyon. When using the word *canyon*, it's normal to think about walking down and in, but in this case we were at the base of the canyon, so we were going to be walking up. As we began walking, I immediately noticed that the canyon floor where we were walking was not steep, as I expected; in fact, it was a very comfortable and gradual incline, with beautiful red rock and limestone walls on both sides, and the place felt very inviting and safe. At the base of the canyon, where we currently were, it was wide and open on either side, but I could tell that the canyon was going to gradually get narrower as we walked up and into it, as the sheer canyon walls came together little by little.

A few minutes later, we came to a bend in the canyon, and I stopped walking to take a good look around. What I saw was astounding—not in some mysterious or mystical way, but in the most tangible way possible: I was suddenly surrounded by almost every species of plant, cactus, bush, and tree that grows in the Sedona chaparral. The feeling of life all around me was incredible, and the realization that I had found a very special place was beginning to dawn on me. I know the flora of this part of the country very well, and that only enhanced the special qualities of this canyon, as I knew that it was not at all common to see pine growing next to cypress growing next to manzanita growing next to prickly pear growing next to agave growing next to banana yucca growing next to barrel cactus growing next to scrub oak growing next to holly growing next to basket yucca growing next to desert sage growing next to chaparral amargosa growing next to mormon tea growing next to cholla growing next to cat's claw growing next to soaptree yucca growing next to juniper growing next to ocotillo growing next to mesquite growing next to datura (which is also known as devil's weed) ... Sure, all these species live in the desert chaparral, but *never* had I seen them all growing together. This part of the canyon was as diverse as any arboretum I'd ever visited.

The feeling of sacredness and the interconnection of all life oozed from this natural arboretum, and I felt my consciousness shifting into an altered state that was in intimate connection with all that was around me. Walking further into the canyon simply increased this sense of heightened awareness until, about a mile into the canyon, I was overcome by the distinct feeling that I was being watched.

It wasn't so much that I simply felt I was being watched—that was an expected feeling for the altered state I was in—but rather it was the sheer intensity of the feeling that raised the hair on my arms and sent goose bumps up and down my body. The feeling was so intense that I decided, right then and there, before continuing any further, to sit with that feeling and try to figure out what exactly was going on. It didn't take long to realize that even though the feeling of being watched was almost overwhelming to the point of my actually being afraid, I wasn't afraid at all. The feeling was not threatening, like if there were a cougar watching me or someone was hiding with a gun, ready to jump me.

So, with the clarity that I wasn't in any immediate danger, I kept walking, the canyon kept growing narrower, and within another half-mile, it finally hit me. It was the cypress trees! They had gradually become thicker and more dense on either side of me as I walked up and back into the canyon, until now I was standing in a sea of them. Their purplish and gray bark glistened in the sun and shadows, and their unusual quality of straight, twisting, and curving growth gave them a surreal and mystical quality I'd never experienced before with this type of tree. And they were definitely watching me, making sure of my intentions. Without another thought, I offered a prayer of intention:

Grandfather Fire
Grandmother Growth
Mother Earth
Father Sun
Sister Water
Brother Wind

All the beings that live in this place, both seen and unseen.
We come here today in humbleness and gratitude, to take only
memories and maybe a few photos, and to leave only footprints.
We ask that you help open our hearts, our minds, our bodies, and our
spirits to receive whatever it is that you have to share with us today.
And when we return to this spot in a little while, may we be
safe, happy, and maybe a little bit wiser. Gracias.

With my prayer of intention that I was there to commune and not to harm now stated out loud to the beings and spirits of the place, the energy surrounding me seemed to open in a way that made me feel more accepted in the place and more at ease, even though I knew they were still watching my actions.

I casually walked farther into the canyon, admiring the beauty of the red rock cliffs with yellow and whitish streaks drawing closer to me as I walked. I suddenly realized this was a box canyon, a canyon that ends (or begins) with steep cliffs on three sides, so there's only one way in and one way out. Immediately, my heart started to race, because many of the best ancient sites I had discovered in the past were located in the "box" of a hidden box canyon.

This time would prove to be unforgettable. When I reached the end of the canyon and could go no farther, I looked up at the cliff face to my right and there, sitting under a large overhang of rock, was one of the most well-preserved cliff dwellings I had ever found. I climbed up to it, and it was nearly perfect, even though it was probably around 1,000 to 1,500 years old. The stacked rocks that formed the half-moon-shaped dwelling, with its back to the cliff face, were so expertly placed, and the overhang of the cliff provided such good protection from the weather, that this ancient dwelling had survived the years miraculously well.

Actually, too well. It suddenly occurred to me just how "protected" this place really was, especially in a metaphysical sense. Most other cliff dwellings not protected as official historic sites had long ago been ruined by the white settlers of the region during their conflicts with the Indians. Even with the superb building skills of the ancient people and the physical protection of the cliff's overhang, for this structure to have survived this long completely intact was nothing less than a miracle—especially considering that it was only a few miles from the town of Sedona, and I knew of not one person who knew of this place. This was not simply an ancient cliff dwelling, it was a supremely sacred site with powerful agents of protection watching over it.

I wanted to spend the night there but I hadn't brought adequate provisions for either Sophie or myself, so after a nice long visit with the place and a ceremony with Grandfather Fire, I said goodbye and thank you to the place and headed for home with an incredible feeling of having just been granted access to a place few people will probably ever see. During the next few years, I visited and spent the night many times while developing a deep connection to the place. It continues to be one of my most precious sacred sites on the planet, even more so because of what happened a few months after I first discovered it.

I was having a chat one day with a Hopi friend and his grandfather, whom I had just met. The grandfather was a wise old medicine man who created amazingly fine artwork from wood, especially his handmade flutes and pipes. The medicine man and I were chatting about different ancient sacred sites in the area when in one moment I realized we were talking about my "secret" canyon.

He said, "Hum, so you've been there?"

"Yes, many times."

"So they let you in, did they?"

"What do you mean?" I asked.

"You know what I mean."

"The cypresses?"

"Of course! They don't let just anyone go back in that canyon. That place is protected by its guardians. You must have a clean heart, a deep connection to nature, and make darn sure you tell them what you are doing there before they will let you into the back of that canyon and into the ancient sacred site."

Well, I must admit that even though I had felt exactly what the old medicine man was saying, and I wanted to believe what he was telling me, there was still a bit of doubt in me. Rationally speaking, if a person with any experience hiking in the wilderness were to find that canyon, on a physical level all you have to do is keep walking toward the back of the canyon until it ends at the box. Simple...

But my doubts about the protection of the place were completely extinguished over the next couple of years. In this day and age, nothing can be kept completely secret, so I have seen with my own eyes experienced hikers who found out about the secret canyon coming back down into the base of the canyon all scratched up, sweating, and huffing and puffing after getting turned around in that canyon while searching for the sacred site. I have run into them on their way out of the canyon and they ask me, "Can you show us where the ancient cliff dwelling is back here? We've been searching and searching and can't find it." Of course, I politely tell them that I can't, because it's not up to me. It's up to the guardians...

◆ ● ◆

Uxmal

While visiting the city of Mérida on the Yucatan peninsula of Mexico, one afternoon I sat eating lunch in the outdoor courtyard of a restaurant near to the center of the city. To my delight, a troupe of native Mayan dancers all dressed up in traditional regalia gave an extravagant performance of ancient dances for the tourists in return for monetary donations.

When the dance concluded, the troupe all gathered for a rest outside of the courtyard, and as I was leaving I struck up a conversation with one of the male dancers. His name was Chon, and he appeared to be in his mid-twenties. I was immediately struck by his quick wit, smile, and jovial manner. We talked and joked around for about twenty minutes, and then while the troupe was packing up to leave, he invited me to come with them to Uxmal, an ancient archeological site about an hour away where they were going to perform that night. Since I was planning to visit Uxmal anyway,

I jumped at the chance. They were going to take the bus there, but I squeezed as many of them as I could into my rental SUV to save them money, and Chon rode in front with me.

Upon arriving at Uxmal, the dancers set up on the side of the main pyramid, named the Temple of the Magician. The archeological site is very popular, and as it began to get dark, a large group of tourists assembled on the stone benches next to the courtyard to watch the show, which included an incredible light show on and around the pyramid that was accompanied by a narrative about the history of the site in addition to dancing. I had been to Uxmal a few times before with friends and had seen the show before, but this time, being in the company of the dancers, it was a completely new experience, and I felt a deep sense of connection to the place.

Afterwards, Chon asked where I was going to stay that night, and when I told him I wasn't sure, he immediately invited me to come to their village that was not far away and to stay with them. I was overjoyed and accepted his generous invitation. We had a light meal and then went to bed at a time for me that was very early, but when my head hit the pillow I fell right to sleep.

The next day was relaxed. Chon and I took a long but leisurely walk through the jungle, and he taught me a lot about the native plants and animals that inhabited the region. As we arrived back at the village near nightfall, Chon asked me if I *really* wanted to experience the mysteries of Uxmal. "We call it the place of miracles, and if you are open to it, you may find out why," Chon said in mysterious voice that I had not heard him use before. Knowing the power of voice from my Huichol mentors, I suddenly realized that the jovial Chon was immensely more than he appeared to be…

Just after midnight, we arrived at the Pyramid of the Magician, climbed the steep steps almost to the top, and sat comfortably on a wide ledge just below the top section of the pyramid. Looking to my left, I saw a giant iguana laying on the ledge not twenty feet from us, and immediately I got the distinct feeling of the magic of the pyramid that I had not experienced previously.

Chon obviously intuited what I was feeling and said, "We call this the place of miracles for many reasons. Most people don't realize this, but unlike many ancient pyramids, there is no quarry anywhere near here for the stone that was necessary for its construction. So where did the stone come from, and how did it get here? There are also no rivers or springs or cenotes to provide water, unlike other sites connected to this one, such as the famous Chichen Itza. So why did my ancient ancestors build a large city, that at one time had 25,000 people, in the middle of a dense jungle with no water supply?"

I looked at him quizzically and admitted I had no answer to either question. "The answer is twofold," Chon continued. "First, the people relied entirely on rain for their water, and the shamans here at Uxmal were in direct contact with the rain god Chac. His figure is carved into the rock of this pyramid in many places. They would pray to Chac, and he would fill the cisterns with the life-giving water. Without Chac, the people would die or have to leave here. But they didn't worry about that because they were in such close relation with Chac. However, the main reason for building in this place is the powerful energy contained in the earth just underneath this pyramid. The ancient shamans were very attuned to the energies of the earth, and right here they found a super-high energy emanating from deep in the ground.

"The ancient legends say that this pyramid was originally created by a magical dwarf in just one night. My ancestors built over the original structure five times throughout many centuries, but this you already know from the archeologists.

"Long ago in Kabah, near to here, an old and powerful witch wanted a child but was not able to conceive, so by magic she brought forth a baby boy from an egg. Everyone was astounded because the boy matured into an adult and even had a beard after only a few days. But he never grew to full height; he was a dwarf. One day, while his mom was out, he found a magic gong that the old witch had carefully hidden. He hit the gong many times, and it could be heard throughout the kingdom. It frightened the King of Uxmal, as there was an ancient prophecy which predicted that when this ancient gong was heard throughout the kingdom, a new king would challenge him for the throne. In fear of losing his position, the king found the dwarf and challenged him to a number of tests and physical feats. The dwarf equaled the king in all the tests, and the king became extremely angry and humiliated that a dwarf could match him, so he challenged him to one last test.

"The last test required the dwarf to endure the pain of a cocoyol (a hard fruit) being broken on his head. The dwarf accepted the challenge, with the condition that if *he* passed the test, he would break a cocoyol on the king's head. Little did the king know that the old witch had concealed a flint headpiece under her son's hair, so the dwarf survived. When the dwarf hit the cocoyol on the king's head, it shattered his skull and he died immediately. The dwarf was now the new king, and since that time this place has been a center of magic and a school of the mysterious.

"It is said that the first thing the dwarf did as the new king was magically erect three pyramids in one night: the Palace of the Governor to serve as his ruling palace, the House of the Old Woman for his mother the witch, and the Temple of the Magician for himself.

"My grandfather has been the shaman of our village for over fifty years but is very old now, and since I was born he has been teaching me the ancient ways, and one day I will take his place. He taught me when I was a small child how to talk to the magic dwarf that we call Itzamna. Itzamna is the god of the heavens and creation. My grandfather says that the dwarf is but a tiny offshoot of the great god Itzamna that the old witch somehow pulled off from him. I have spoken to him hundreds of times, and he has always answered all of my questions except for one. Whenever I ask him if he really did create the three structures magically all in one night, he simply smiles but does not answer... Do you want to try and speak with him?"

"Sure," I said with an uneasy feeling growing inside me.

"Okay. Stand up, Jim."

Chon produced a large cigar that I immediately recognized as the sacred tobacco *Nicotiana rustica*, which the Maya grow to smoke during ceremonies. This sacred tobacco is twenty times stronger than regular tobacco. Chon proceeded to smudge me with the smoke by taking large puffs on the cigar and blowing it all over my body to cleanse my energy field. Then he pulled a large brown egg from his bag, cracked the egg on the stone, and placed the yolk gently on the ledge we were on. He proceeded to chant in his language while tapping on a small gong he had brought with him. When that was done, he told me to sit quietly and wait.

A few moments later, I heard Chon say words of greeting in his language. "Do you see him?" asked Chon. I looked all around but saw nothing unusual. "He's sitting right there—where I cracked the egg," Chon said in a whisper.

I couldn't see the dwarf and was beginning to wonder if Chon was pulling my leg. But he simply shrugged his shoulders, and for the next twenty minutes or so I listened to one side of a conversation he was supposedly having with the spirit of the dwarf king. He spoke in his own language, so I didn't understand what he was saying.

Then Chon stood up and said it was time to leave. "We can try again tomorrow night, if you like."

"Okay," I replied skeptically. "But what about the egg?"

"The iguana will take care of that."

For the next three nights, we repeated the same procedure at the pyramid, with the same results. I was feeling like I would never get to speak with or see the magical dwarf. Chon said it was okay, that he had received special instructions from the dwarf king, and that he was confident I would meet him the following night.

The next night, we followed the same procedure except before cracking the egg, Chon handed me a small hand-rolled cigar. "My grandfather has prepared this special mixture for you, Jim. Inside the cigar is the dried powder excretions from the sacred toad of the jungle. This will help you to meet with Itzamna."

I had read about cultures using toad secretions to achieve visionary experiences but also that they could be very dangerous. Chon read my mind and calmly said, "Not to worry, Jim; for years beyond count, my family has raised hundreds of generations of this particular toad. It is the only species of toad that can lead you to Itzamna. The other types of toads can be harmful, but this one is a sacred ally and almost impossible to find in the jungle anymore. Maybe there are none left in the wild—I have never seen one. But my grandfather has about thirty of them that he keeps in a large fenced-in area next to his hut. He takes wonderful care of them. They are very happy to live with us, and that's why they help us when we ask."

Chon broke the egg and carefully laid the yolk beside us, being careful not to break the yolk. He instructed me to sit and smoke half of the cigar and beat slowly on the gong while saying my own prayer to the dwarf king and invite him to join us. I did as he said.

With the first puff of the cigar, my whole body began to tingle. By the time I had smoked half the cigar and put it out, I was seeing a kaleidoscope of colors and geometric figures looking out over the jungle's canopy. "Look at the egg," Chon said quietly.

I looked beside us and standing there, staring at me, was the dwarf king! He looked old but not ancient. He was only about four feet tall and had a long, silver beard with very dark brown skin, and he was dressed in a simple white tunic. "Greetings, young man," the dwarf king said to me jovially in English. I couldn't speak, but even if I could I would have had no words.

He seemed to know what I was experiencing. He held out a hand to me and, with a loud laugh, said, "Come with me!"

I took his hand, and we walked right into the pyramid. I felt myself passing through the different layers of the pyramid and slowly sinking down into the very base of the structure. We ended up in a small room where a small fire was magically burning, with no fuel for the fire to be seen anywhere. He sat me down on a small bench next to the fire and sat next to me. The colorful geometric patterns were still floating all around but not as intensely as before. His powerful and extraordinary presence seemed to be focusing my attention entirely on him.

"Welcome to the temple of magic, Jim," the dwarf king said kindly. With that said, my voice seemed to naturally come back to me, and we had a long conversation. He was a peculiarly curious fellow and asked me many questions about what was going on in the outside world and with my life, even though I had the distinct impression that he already knew all that I was telling him.

Seemingly satisfied with the conversation and laughing at many things I didn't even consider to be funny, he casually poured a mug of strong coffee from a pot I hadn't noticed by the fire and handed it to me.

Sipping his own coffee, he asked, "Do you believe in magic, Jim?"

"I certainly know there are many things I have experienced that I can't explain with my rational mind, including this," I replied.

"It's very good you realize that, because the magic I am talking about is not the parlor-trick variety, Jim. It is brought about by the power and magic of intention. Your intentions create your reality. You already know this, but you have not yet fully conceived of the power in this statement. Especially from now on, since you will be taking the magic and energy of this place with you when you leave, you must be very careful with your thoughts, what you say to yourself and others, what you write, and everything you do. You have the power to create or destroy. You must use your power wisely and with thought of how your actions and words will affect everything around you."

Just as he finished saying that, a flash of the view I had looking over the jungle while sitting on the pyramid's ledge with Chon flickered in front of my eyes. "Our time together is almost done, Jim. Be mindful of what I said, and come back anytime! I used to have many friends come visit me. But throughout the centuries, they came less and less. Now I only have a couple left. Most of the people these days don't believe in magic and therefore can't see me or don't want to."

"Can I ask you one last question?" I asked.

"Of course."

"How can you possibly know how to speak English?"

"I told you! It's MAGIC!"

With that, he threw his arms in the air, and the next thing I knew, I was sitting next to Chon on the ledge. I felt like myself again, although I was a little tired, and I told Chon all that happened. "That's good advice he gave you, Jim." I agreed, and we walked back to the village in silence. I have been back twice since then, but unlike Chon I still need the help of the toads to meet with the dwarf king.

Since that first experience with the dwarf king, something has changed inside me, and I have found a deeper realization of how my thoughts and actions affect not only me but everyone and everything around me, both seen and unseen. And it goes without saying that I have a new understanding of the word *magic* and how it manifests with every thought and action in my life.

———◆◆———

Huiricuta

The land of Huiricuta is one of the most sacred places on earth to my Huichol mentors as well as myself. Huiricuta lies within the Chihuahuan Desert in the state of San Luis Potosi, Mexico. The Chihuahuan Desert is arguably the most biologically diverse desert region in the world; it is rivaled only by the Great Sandy Desert of Australia and the Namib-Karoo in South Africa. The Chihuahuan Desert is home to more than 3,000 plant species, 120 reptile species, 25 amphibian species, and 250 bird species, as well as a unique variety of aquatic species. It contains around 30 percent of the world's cacti species, a great number of which can be found nowhere else on the planet. In 1994, Conservación Humana and the WWF (World Wildlife Fund) helped the Huichol transform a portion of the Chihuahuan Desert that includes the sacred area of Huiricuta into the Natural Reserve of Huiricuta, an area protected under Mexican environmental legislation. Six years later, this led to the area given the status of "Sacred Gift": within the WWF-ARC (Alliance of Religions and Conservation) international list of sacred gifts for the new millennium, the reserve was enlarged to nearly double—from 74,000 to 140,000 hectares (about 346,000 acres)—and a concrete management plan was put into place. The cooperation between nonprofit groups, the state of San Luis Potosi, and the Huichol elders has resulted in the unprecedented status for Huiricuta's designation as a legal reserve for both ecological and cultural/spiritual preservation.

The first few times I went to the sacred land of Huiricuta, I was invited by Huichol friends whose extended families were going to make the arduous 1,600-kilometer pilgrimage. Depending on the family, the shaman leader of the pilgrimage, and the circumstances, the pilgrimage either starts on the west coast at a sacred site called Jaramara, near the bottom of the Gulf of California, or in the Western Sierra Madres, where the core ceremonial centers and villages of the Huichol still thrive, hidden in the mountains, without roads, electricity, or plumbing. In either case, there are many sacred sites along the pilgrimage route where the pilgrims stop to make offerings and converse and be blessed by the spirits of the various sacred sites along the way. Many ceremonies and rituals are done upon arriving to Huiricuta, and then the hunting and gathering of the sacred peyote cactus commences. The peyote is brought back to their mountain villages for use in the annual calendar of ceremonies performed throughout the year. Although my experiences of making the pilgrimage with families that I have known for many years were unbelievably profound in terms of the impact they had on my view of the world and both my spiritual and personal development, making the pilgrimage with the Huichol jicareros (a group of twenty to thirty men chosen by the elders to serve five years as keepers of the Huichol spiritual traditions) raised the experience to the highest level imaginable.

The main difference between the two styles of making the pilgrimage is that the family pilgrimage is not required to follow all of the traditions regarding the pilgrimage, such as visiting all the sacred sites, singing all the sacred chants, and performing every single little nuance of the tradition. That is what the jicareros are charged with doing. The jicareros are led by at least three head shamans and a number of elders who are responsible for the extensive cycle of yearly ceremonies that make up the arduous Huichol ceremonial calendar. When someone becomes a jicarero, their normal life is basically over for five years. Everything revolves around being a jicarero. From sunrise to bedtime, every day the jicarero's life is filled with ceremony, work in the sacred fields, pilgrimages to sacred places, making offerings, and dozens of other obligations that keep the tradition alive. Not many tewaris (outsiders) have ever gone on the pilgrimage to Huiricuta with the elders and jicareros of the core ceremonial centers. For five years in a row, I went with the jicareros on the three- to four-week pilgrimage to Huiricuta. Words are ultimately inadequate to describe those experiences. The preparation, the sacrifice, the attention to detail in every sacred site and ceremony along the pilgrimage route as well as in Huiricuta and in the collecting of the sacred peyote cactus, on top of many days' fasting or with very little food and hardly any sleep, foster an altered state of consciousness and reverence for the interconnection of all life that is truly a separate reality from the rational-based reality of Western culture.

There are many reasons why the jicareros make the pilgrimage to Huiricuta, the main three being (1) honoring the sacred sites and communing with the spirits of each place along the route; (2) the passing down of the traditions from generation to generation (the Huichol have no written language, although most speak Spanish as their second language); and (3) finding their tasks in life through the visions acquired with the peyote (*hukuri* in Huichol), the sacred fire (Tataiwari), and the magical blue deer (*Kahullumari*) that lives in Huiricuta. Since I am not Huichol, my main reasons for making the pilgrimages were to enhance my knowledge of shamanic practices, to receive visions and messages for how to live my life, and to support the Huichol with the expenses required to make the trip. From my many years of living and working with the Huichol, I eventually gained their trust to the point that I also became the designated photographer of the pilgrimages I went on. I always make a packet of pictures for each jicarero and send them to the ceremonial center when I get home. Adhering to the promise I made, I have never published in any of my books or magazine articles any of the thousands of photographs I have taken while with the Huichol.

The story I would like to share with you is a very brief recounting of my meetings with five of the sacred blue deer of Huiricuta while on pilgrimages with the Huichol jicareros, as these meetings demonstrate what can happen inside an ancient shamanic tradition and how these experiences have the power to enhance one's life.

It was the second night after hunting and gathering the sacred peyote, and all the jicareros were gathered around the sacred fire, cleaning the peyote that would be eaten that night. We had all been traveling for more than a week and purposefully eating little or no food, getting very little sleep, and had two full days of hunting and gathering the peyote in the heavy winds of the desert chaparral. But spirits were extremely high, the hunt had been good, and I prepared myself for another night of visions with the peyote, the fire, and the shaman's chanting.

Very late that night, the shaman took a break from chanting, and all the jicareros, including myself, sat in silence in a circle around the fire in a deep dream state, as all of us had eaten a large amount of the sacred peyote throughout the night. Each of us was on a personal journey into the numinous realms, and a wave of gratitude passed through me that I was fortunate to be part of such a powerful and ancient tradition. I actually felt a sense of pride flowing through me as I realized how special it was to be there in that sacred place with those sacred people and included in their sacred ceremony.

As soon as that feeling of pride and the associated thought flowed through me, I heard something moving behind me. In my deep trance state, I would normally not be motivated to look and see what it was that was making the noise, and subconsciously I knew that I was being protected by the fire, the shaman, and the jicareros, but nonetheless I turned around and saw a most spectacular sight.

The blue deer stepped out of the bushes and walked right up to me. It was glowing almost as bright as the fire. For a few moments I just stared, not really able to do anything more than that. Then I turned to look at the rest of the jicareros, but they all were still sitting and all had their heads bowed, chin on chest. The shaman looked up at me for just a second and then went back to his chin-on-chest trance. With an almost involuntary movement, I stood up and faced the magical blue deer who was standing just a few feet from me.

The blue deer looked down at the ground between us and seemed to be staring intently at something. When I looked down, I almost gasped in surprise, because the deer had somehow written in the rocky, sandy soil *I am third*.

I read the words and had the strong feeling that I had heard or maybe read those same exact words before, but I couldn't put my finger on where or when. At first, I thought the message was about the deer and that the deer was trying to tell me something about itself. But with those thoughts I immediately heard the blue deer speaking to me inside my mind. The deer began to explain to me that the message was for me—that she was the blue deer of humility, and the message was about how to live my life. She said that we can have pride in the things that we accomplish, but that too much pride is self-centeredness, that I needed to be more humble in the face of this mysterious world. If I was truly to become a medicine man and healer for my own people, I needed to surrender to the Great Spirit (God) and do the Great Spirit's work first. Secondly was my service to others. And I was third...

Our eyes met, and the next thing I remember was waking up to the jica-reros packing their gear. Beside me was my notebook, and sometime during the night I had sketched a crude drawing of the blue deer that I had no rec-ollection of doing. I looked over at one of the head shamans, and he smiled knowingly but said not a word. Although I can't claim to have taken the blue deer's advice on humility in all my actions since then, I do try to live her message that I am third, and I will never forget it.

The second year with the jicareros on the pilgrimage to Huiricuta was the last one for this group's cycle of five years of service to the ceremonial cen-ter, so it was especially intense. All of these men had almost completed their five years of service; for some of them, this was their second or third time serving for five years, so even the youngest of the jicareros was inti-mately familiar with all the ceremonies and sacred sites. After the first day of hunting and gathering the peyote in Huiricuta, we were collecting fire-wood as the sun was setting, and in my mind I fully expected that I would have a vision of the blue deer that night with the fire and the peyote I would be eating. But the blue deer did not appear that night. I knew from hearing many stories about the blue deer that it could be a trickster, so the following night before eating the peyote I reminded myself to be on the alert and that the blue deer might simply appear in a different way this time.

Turns out I was right and wrong. The blue deer did appear, and in a similar way as the first time, but this time it was a male deer, and right before my eyes he changed into a huge cougar. Even though I was squarely in the magical time of the peyote, I can still remember thinking to myself how unusual it was: a cougar's main diet in those desert mountains was deer! And with that thought, the giant cat snarled at me, and I became paralyzed. All thoughts stopped, and my body went rigid as an oak tree.

"I am the deer of respect and have chosen this form because I knew you would respect it, for deep respect is what you lack," I heard the cougar talking in my mind. "Oh, you no doubt think you have respect for others, and in some cases you do, but you have not yet embraced the grander scheme of respect. I'm going to tell you a little story.

"I am the king of this desert and these mountains. If the antelope or the deer catch sight of me crouching in the bush, they do not forget to run. The coyote steer clear of me, other cougars avoid me, even the mighty humans with their guns are afraid of me. You are afraid of me. Yes, I am the most feared and respected of the animals here.

"That is why I became so angry when this annoying little creature interrupted my sleep one day. I was lying in some bushes, sleeping, and this tiny mouse came running and hit me right in the nose. I opened my eyes and the mouse froze, knowing I would eat him for a snack, but before I could he said, 'Oh, mighty king, I am terribly sorry—I did not mean to run into you! I wasn't watching where I was going; please forgive me!'

"'You have showed your king respect with your words, and I will not eat you this time,' I answered.

"'Thank you, thank you, thank you,' said the mouse. 'I hope one day to be of service to you for your kindness.'

"I simply laughed at the thought—how could a tiny little mouse ever help me with anything?

"Then one day I wasn't paying close enough attention to where I was walking and fell into a large pit that the humans had dug and covered in order to trap animals to eat. I tried to get out, but they also had a net in there, and the more I struggled, the more tangled I became. After a while, all the other animals heard what had happened, and they came to the edge of the pit and laughed at me. The coyote came by and said that in the morning the hunters would come back and skin me.

"I struggled all night to get free, but it was no use. I was exhausted and finally gave up. A few minutes later, a little pink nose appeared above me. 'Now is my time to repay you, mighty king,' said the little mouse.

"'I am grateful for your good intentions, little mouse,' I replied. 'But there's nothing you can do. Soon the men will come, and there will be a new king, for I shall be dead.'

"With that, the little mouse ran away, but within minutes, dozens of the mouse's family members and friends came, and in their combined effort they gnawed through the net and set me free.

"And that is how I, the king of the animals, learned to respect others. It doesn't matter if you are mighty or meek, quick or slow, beautiful or ugly. Everything deserves respect for what they are. Everything has power of its own measure. This is what you must learn, Jim."

With that, the cougar turned, and as he walked away, he transformed back into a blue deer and disappeared into the night.

My next encounter with the blue deer was the following year and with a whole new group of jicareros. Some of the new jicareros were irritated at being chosen, because it placed so much demand on them and their families. I had seen this before with new jicareros, but always after the five years of service they are completely changed, and I knew it would be the same with this group, and so did the elders and shaman leading the pilgrimage. But at that moment there was still tension in the group, and I found it more difficult to stay focused during the pilgrimage. However, upon arriving at Huiricuta, everyone was happy. No Huichol can be in Huiricuta and *not* be happy, no matter what is happening in the outside world. The sacred land of Huiricuta is in their blood.

On that pilgrimage, I met the deer of perseverance. He walked right out of the sacred fire and, like the second deer, he taught me his lesson with a story.

"At the top of the sacred mountain above us is the town of Real de Catorce, and as you know, that town was built because more than 200 years ago, the humans found silver there and some became very rich. Once there were two poor brothers that were mining for silver. They dug shafts deep into the roots of the mountains, breathing noxious airs and trying to survive floods and cave-ins. They hauled out the ore with their own bodies, climbing crude ladders of notched logs, carrying the heavy loads in the same blankets with which they wrapped themselves at night. For some time they were rewarded with the precious silver, but one day they found their luck had run out. They tried for a few more weeks but found nothing. Finally, in disgust and swearing at the mountain, they gave up and sold all their equipment and their claim for a few hundred dollars and went home with their tails between their legs.

"The man they sold their claim to was smart, and he hired an engineer, who advised him to keep digging where the brothers had left off, and just three feet deeper he found a massive amount of the precious silver. With a little more perseverance and persistence, the brothers would have been rich beyond their wildest dreams.

"How much further within yourself must you dig, Jim? Do you have the perseverance to uncover your true self and the riches that lie within you?"

The blue deer walked into the fire and left me pondering his story and his questions...

My fourth deer must have known about the struggles I would be facing in my life the following year; it was a tough year but throughout it all, I remembered the blue deer of perseverance, and it gave me strength, which leads to my fourth pilgrimage with the jicareros, the second pilgrimage to Huiricuta for this group. A pattern was emerging with my encounters with the deer, as once again the lesson was delivered with a story, and of course the story and the lesson were perfect for my current life situation:

Looking me straight in the eye, the female deer began. "Once there was a teenage boy who went to town with his grandfather. In the small Mexican town was a store that sold all sorts of things and also would make trades with the customers. The boy saw an old watch in a case and fell in love with it. Being a Huichol who lived in the mountains, he did not have any need for a watch, but nonetheless he asked his grandfather if he would buy it for him. It was not expensive, but most Huichol had very little money, as they lived off the land and their crops. Even though his grandfather had the money from selling some of his artwork, he told the boy no, but that if he worked real hard doing chores for his neighbors maybe he could earn enough pesos to buy it. The boy worked real hard, and in a few weeks he had the pesos and bought the cheap watch.

"Even though it didn't keep good time and he really didn't need it, he wore it everywhere and never took it off. He saw that a few of the elders of the village had watches because they had to deal with the world outside of their mountains to keep their villages safe and at times travel to the big city to talk and make agreements with the government.

"The boy's grandfather was a wise old elder who was one of the few that would at times travel to the big city, but he didn't have a watch. What he did have was thousands of stories, and each night he would tell one around the fire after the family had eaten and before going to bed. One night after the story, the grandfather came into the boy's room as the boy lay in his bed ready to sleep. 'Do you love me?' the grandfather asked. 'Of course I do,' replied the boy. 'Then give me your watch,' the grandfather said. 'Oh, no—not my watch, Grandfather! But you can have my machete, it's a really good one.' The grandfather just smiled. 'That's okay, I already have a machete; you get some sleep now.'

"The next week, the grandfather came to the boy's room again and asked, 'Do you love me, grandson?' The boy replied, 'You know I do, Grandfather.' And again the grandfather said, 'Then give me your watch.' The boy replied. 'Oh, no—not my watch! But you can have these beads for your artwork.' The grandfather told the boy he already had enough beads and wished the boy good dreams as he left.

"The following week, the grandfather came once again to the boy's room. The boy was sitting on the bed and extended his hand to his grandfather. In his hand was his watch. With a grin as big as the ocean, the grandfather took the watch with one hand and with the other handed the boy a small, fancy box containing a brand-new watch."

The blue deer of sacrifice opened my eyes to the illusion of thinking that I have things I absolutely need to hold on to. What new treasures of life would I open myself up to if I were able to let them go?

This story ends with my fifth pilgrimage to Huiricuta. One of the head shamans of the jicareros was the father of my best Huichol friend, and I knew him well—or I should say well enough for an American to know a Huichol shaman. Anyway, after the long days of traveling to Huiricuta and before the hunting and gathering of the peyote, he and the other shamans and elders pulled me aside and explained to me, much to my disbelief, that I was not to hunt the peyote this time, nor was I to take it into my body. They explained that there comes a time when we must learn our lessons through our own inner light and connection to the Great Spirit—that I was to go to a sacred hill away from the jicareros and stay there, fasting, for five days while the jicareros did their hunting.

They took me to the hill as the jicareros watched me leaving and shouted blessings and good fortune, as they obviously knew what I was to do. When we got to the sacred hill, I was far from the jicareros, somewhere in Huiricuta I had never been, and I doubted if I could have found my way back on my own. A sudden fear swept over me, and the old shaman began to explain, "This is where you must use everything you have learned in Huiricuta, Jim. Only by successfully completing this task will you truly become a medicine man for your people. Throughout the years, the blue deer of Huiricuta have given you lessons about humility, respect, perseverance, and sacrifice. The fifth deer you must encounter without eating the peyote. The peyote spirit is all around you here, as you know, but you must not eat it. You must try and connect with it and everything around you on your own."

Another even older shaman then said, "This is where you shall sit, with no view of roads or fences; with no blanket to sit on, you feel the earth; with no fire, you shiver for your vision and look into the darkness. You slowly become the rocks, the plants, the bushes, the animals. Here, you become an animal; nothing more, nothing less. We will come back for you at sunrise after your fifth night." And with that, they left, and I was all alone in the sacred desert of Huiricuta.

Space does not allow for the telling of all that happened during that five days, but one of the first things I learned was that I was not alone. During my days and nights, I was visited by the coyote and fox, rabbit and snake, vulture and eagle. I could feel the peyote all around me as if watching. On the third night, the wind blew so strong that as I sat there, shivering, I was covered with sand and by morning was barely distinguishable from my surroundings. The boredom of sitting in that one place with thoughts of the jicareros wandering free during their hunts and the bonding of stories and chants by the night fire was almost unbearable. My stomach felt like it was eating itself, but by far it was thirst that was driving me crazy. I had fasted before on vision quests in the wild, but never without water. Those days in Huiricuta pushed and tested me way beyond anything I had ever done before.

At dawn after the fifth night, I heard something coming up the hill, but it was not the shaman, as I had expected. It was my fifth blue deer. Barely able to sit up and look at the deer, he started his story:

"Once there was a Huichol man about your age that was an expert archer and won all the contests. He was boastful and arrogant about his skill and one day challenged an elder of the tribe who was well known as their greatest hunter and had no use for competitions. The archer hit the bull's-eye on the first shot and with the second shot split his own arrow. 'See that, old man? Try and beat me!'

"The elder simply smiled knowingly but did not shoot. He motioned for the archer to follow him and walked away. The archer was puzzled but curious, so he followed along for many miles until they came to a deep gorge with a swift running river way down below them. Spanning the chasm was a flimsy log someone had placed there to cross, and the elder very calmly and nimbly made his way to the center of the chasm, aimed his arrow at a faraway tree, and made a direct hit. 'Now it's your turn,' he said as he casually walked back on the shaky log.

"Looking into the seemingly bottomless abyss, the archer shook with terror and anger, and he could not force himself to step out onto the log, much less shoot at a target. 'You have much skill with your bow,' the elder said. 'But you have little skill over the mind that lets loose the shot.'"

"You see, Jim," said the blue deer to me in the predawn light, "both the archer and the elder had skill, but the elder also had wisdom. I am the deer of wisdom, and my message to you is that wisdom is the antidote for arrogance, impatience, anger, and ignorance. Wisdom is the sum of our experiences; the ups and downs, highs and lows, successes and failures. Wisdom comes from the light and from the darkness; from the level of perception that only comes from experience and through our struggles. You have faced this task, this struggle, very well, and now you have its experience and the wisdom it teaches. Now, would you like a drink of water?"

Upon trying to stand up and answer the magical deer that YES! I would give anything for some water, I took my eyes off the deer, and when I looked back he was gone. But coming up the hill were the shamans to collect me, and of course they gave me a little water.

Life is like riding a bicycle.
To keep your balance
you must keep moving.
ALBERT EINSTEIN

CHAPTER 7

⑭edicine of Healing:
The Journey Continues

———◆———

Shamanic healing rituals and practices, along with the profound importance of offerings and exchanges, are some of the most difficult aspects of shamanism for people outside of a shamanic culture to grasp, and thus they are often the most misunderstood. One of the most accurate and telling ways of comprehending a specific culture's view of the world is exploring how the people define, diagnose, and treat illness and disease. In this sense, it is reasonable to say that balance is the underlying theme to health and sickness in shamanic cultures, as balance is also the foundation of their worldview.

Balance is acquired and maintained through the continual efforts of exchange and reciprocity with both the physical and spiritual worlds. If the delicate balance between humans and the physical-spiritual worlds is disturbed or upset, then people get sick, the environment becomes unhealthy, crops do not grow, people fight or bicker, and suffering in general replaces healthy living. Maintaining balance and correcting imbalances when they occur is thus of primary importance.

In terms of medical treatment (aside from obvious trauma such as broken bones or other physical injuries), the shamanic healer locates the causes of imbalance between the patient's physical and spiritual surroundings and eliminates sickness or disease through restoring healthy balance. There are myriad techniques that shamans employ cross-culturally throughout the world for restoring and maintaining balance. In these final two stories, we dive into one of the powerful shamanic healing practices of the ancestors of the ancient Mazateca-Nahua healers, from whom I have been receiving training for almost two decades. This type of healing uses the powers of dreaming and ritual to clear and restore a person's injured soul.

Spirit Cleansing

For a period of more than a year, I inexplicably felt almost completely out of the flow of my life that I had been accustomed to experiencing. My energy and enthusiasm for life was dramatically lower, there were troubles in my relationships and with loved ones, I had a hard time concentrating, and worst of all, I had started a process of putting things off simply because I didn't feel like doing them. When all of this was happening, I found myself withdrawing into myself, making excuses to not participate in social events, not visiting my sacred places, even not walking with my dog nearly as much. I stayed home a lot, but even there I only took care of the things I absolutely needed to. I was out of balance for sure. The only joy I really had was when I was working with my clients out on the land. For some unexplainable reason, when I was doing that I felt like a totally different person, like my normal self—energetic, confident, outgoing, helpful.

During this time period, I was also having some of the most lucid dreams I had ever had. Almost every morning I would awake in wonderment that I was lying in my bed. My dreams were so real, they didn't feel like dreams at all. Many times upon waking I wouldn't want to even deal with my "real" reality, so instead of getting up I would go back to sleep and enter right back into my dream. I even found myself napping during the day, neglecting the things I should have been doing. Since I was single, had no children, and lived alone, I wasn't really hurting anyone, but deep down I could feel something just wasn't right with me.

Finally, what motivated me to seek answers to my malaise were my dreams themselves. Recurrent places and people filled my dreams on a daily basis to the point that I actually preferred living in my dreams rather than in the waking world. The two most prominent people in my dreams were my father, who had passed away more than thirty years ago, and the mushroom shaman from Oaxaca, Xilonen, both of whom were among the many people I would relate to and talk to in my dreams, just as I would have in the waking world. Finally, I decided that something had to be done, and I instinctively knew what it was. Since my father was no longer alive, I had to talk with Xilonen in person. The problem was that I had no way of contacting her. I tried all the old numbers I had for Armando in Mexico City, but all were a dead end. Finally, a few months later, I arranged to go see Xilonen in person in Oaxaca.

I arrived at the small village to a hero's welcome. A small family feast was held at Soledad's home my first night there, and for a short time I actually forgot what I had come there for. But that night in my dreams I entered a vast cave, and near the back was someone sitting close to a fire. As I got closer, I saw that it was not a person but seemed to be a giant mushroom covered in a shawl. Somehow I knew that it was Xilonen, and I immediately woke up to predawn light entering under my door and the sound of roosters greeting the sun.

Without a second thought, I jumped out of bed and went directly to Xilonen's hut down the way. I banged on the door, but she didn't answer. I went around back but found no one. Suddenly, images of the night I took the mushrooms flashed into my mind, and I found myself running through the woods toward the tree that had protected me that night. About halfway there, I ran into Xilonen and a young teenage girl walking back from the fields with a basket full of the little holy ones. Xilonen simply stopped and said, "What took you so long"—not so much as a question but as a statement. Then, looking me up and down, she added, "Go clean up and come by my house when the night begins to awake," which in her terms meant sunset. Not realizing that I hadn't even tied my shoes or combed my hair and that my zipper was down, I quickly arranged myself and headed back to Soledad's place, where I was staying. That evening, I began a remarkable journey of healing and instruction with the powerful curandera Xilonen.

The first thing Xilonen did was ask for a full account of my dreams. This took almost half the night, and when I finally finished, Xilonen sighed and said that my dreams made it very clear to her that I had two major "winds" blowing inside me. One was an evil wind that was causing the lethargy in my life, and the second was a wind calling me toward the underworld. She explained that the evil wind must be dealt with first, because that one was sucking out my energy, and I would need my full strength to deal with the situation of the underworld. Xilonen said that she would dream for me that night to find out where the evil wind was coming from and asked me for something personal of mine to place on her altar. I took off my rose-bead necklace that I had made with Maggie and Amy and handed it to her. She took the necklace in both hands as if feeling it and then simply smiled and motioned me toward the door.

That was the first night in a very long time that I awoke in the morning without remembering a single dream. I went to the kitchen, and Soledad handed me a cup of coffee. "No time to eat now," she said hurriedly. "Drink up—we have to go to the market right away. Xilonen was here at first light and told me all of the offerings we need for your healing ceremony. I wrote them all down here," she added as she handed me a piece of paper. Soledad also handed me back my necklace. "Xilonen says to wear that all the time—it has powerful medicine and has parts of your soul in it. If you were to lose it, you would lose part of your soul."

The offerings I needed to purchase included tobacco, liquor, candles, and some kind of modern or American type of food. In addition to an American food item, I also had to purchase many traditional food items such as tortillas and ingredients for making a soup, as well as chocolate and soft drinks. The items were easy to obtain, but the only American thing I could find in the small marketplace were lollipops, so I bought the whole bag. Other items that Soledad and I gathered from around her house and the village were copal resin, three different types of flowers, and a black hen and one of her eggs.

I was told that Xilonen would arrive later in the afternoon and would expect that everything was ready when she arrived. Soledad informed me that we would use the living room of her house for the ceremony, because she and her family—her sons and daughters and their wives, husbands, and children—were my sponsors. A little while later, we got back to Soledad's, and there were half a dozen women and children of Soledad's family already at her house. Some began making the soup and tamales, while others dressed up the family altar with flowers and candles and traditional offerings of coffee and cornmeal. Soledad got a brazier and the copal ready.

Just before sundown, Xilonen arrived and, without any formalities, went right to work. First, she checked that all the offerings she had instructed me to get had been gathered, and she put them all together on the right side of the altar. She then made sure the food would be ready. Satisfied all was going smoothly, she asked for a low bench to sit on in front of the altar, placed her handbag on the floor, and began removing stacks of different colors of tissue-type paper. Then, from a large roll that resembled holiday wrapping paper, she carefully cut sections and placed them on the floor between her and the altar.

By this time, most of the rest of Soledad's extended family were there, either watching or helping with something, as well as more than a few people from the village who came to watch (and some to get a free meal). In a few moments, I would understand why Xilonen was so highly respected. Once the "beds" for the spirits were laid down (the cut sheets of decorated paper), Xilonen began to fold and cut the various colors of tissue paper into representations of the spirits she wanted to invoke. I found out later that the folding and cutting of the paper spirits takes many years to master, and that Xilonen was the unrivaled expert not only at folding and cutting the patterns but also in the knowledge and number of spirits she could use in her healing sessions.

With the paper effigies complete, Xilonen called for the food offerings to be brought to the altar and the ceremony to begin. Soledad brought the brazier full of hot coals and the copal to Xilonen. Standing with my back to the altar, she fanned the thick smoke all over my body and then throughout the whole room to cleanse everything and everyone. In the midst of the thick smoke, she grabbed the black hen, and while chanting some prayers swiftly broke its neck and handed it to one of the women to be cooked later. With that done, Xilonen continued her chanting while laying out one by one the paper figures she had cut in an intricate design on the floor on top of the spirit beds. She instructed that the candles be lit, and then, while still chanting, she carefully chose items from the offerings and placed them on top of the cut paper display. Some effigies got soft drinks while others got liquor or food or candle wax dripped onto them. One particular cutout was the only one to receive any of the lollipops, and it had more offerings on it than any of the others, although all the effigies received multiple offerings. (The paper effigy with the lollipops was for the evil wind that was hexing me. Xilonen told me later that the wind had gotten to know me and liked modern American things, so the lollipops were there "to lure him in.")

Xilonen then began reciting the main chant of the healing. First, she named each of the spirits that she was invoking to be rid of, then a list of the offerings to the spirits, and then a plea to the spirits, which is really more like a demand, for the damaging spirits to leave me alone so that I could recover my health and my strength. During this long, low chant, she would sometimes touch the effigies, sometimes place one or two on my forehead or rub them on me, spread more copal smoke all around, and pour soft drinks, liquor, and soup onto the effigies.

With the conclusion of the main chant, I was instructed to move away from the altar, and I joined Soledad near the kitchen entrance. Xilonen then began a different chant and began turning the paper effigies over. Soledad whispered in my ear that Xilonen had captured the spirits by luring them with the copal smoke, candles, and most importantly the offerings that they liked so much and couldn't resist. Now that she had them trapped, she was going to send them away.

After turning all of them over, Xilonen then took a few of the effigies at a time, dramatically tore them to pieces, and then blew on the pieces while commanding the spirits to leave and not come back. When all the effigies had been ripped to shreds, she carefully collected all the soggy pieces of paper, including the scraps from when she had cut the effigies, and placed them in a cloth bundle, which she tied tightly at the top. Soledad told me that Xilonen would hide and bury the bundle somewhere far off in the woods where no one would find it.

Before leaving, Xilonen cleansed me and many of the people with more copal, sacred feathers, flowers, palm leaves, and beeswax. She gave me one of the beeswax candles and told me to keep it lit by my bed all night and to come see her in the morning, as we still had much work to do. I ate some of the food that had been rewarmed and spoke with Soledad briefly before going to bed. I was pretty much in awe of what Xilonen had just done. Words can in no way describe the atmosphere or performance created by a curandera of Xilonen's level.

Soledad casually explained to me, "Xilonen is a powerful and successful healer because she can do battle with dangerous spirits to help her patients restore balance and health. But most people can't see and don't realize how dangerous it is for her while she is doing it. Only those who have traveled to the underworld have any clue what really goes on when a real curandera like Xilonen does her work. You will find this out very soon, I am sure. In the meantime, realize this: most of what people see Xilonen actually doing during a healing ceremony is to create an impact on both the patient and the audience. The more dramatic the impact and the positive impressions of healing, the better for all concerned, even for the healer. But the majority of the work Xilonen has done for you she did last night in her dreams. Today's ceremony was to seal the deal, so to speak. Run along and sleep well tonight, James; you have a date with destiny tomorrow…"

The Cure, the Curer,
and the Underworld

"It's easy to talk of these things while we sit here outside on the patio with the sun shining on us and a nice breeze blowing through our hair and a good, full belly," Xilonen began with a far-off gaze toward the woods and a puff of her cigarette. "But it's a different story altogether when you are in the midst of it. These things we will now speak of.

"From the dreams you have told me about, I now know that you have entered the underworld many times and through various openings. I went to the underworld the night before last to find your *nagual*, your animal spirit, to see if I could help it and thus help you. But going into my dreaming while holding your rose beads, I found something else. In the underworld there was a particular foul spirit that was attracted to me. He came in the form of a man, but I soon found out he wasn't really attracted to me at all—he came to me because I had your necklace, the essence of your blood, with me. That is how I found out that this evil wind had been following you and that someone had placed it on you.

"So tell me, do you know of anyone with the power and knowledge to hex you with an evil wind and why they would do it?"

I could think of plenty of shamans I knew from various cultures that probably could have done it, but I couldn't believe any of them would, and I also couldn't think of any reason why they would. But as Xilonen kept questioning me and narrowing down the criteria, I suddenly remembered a gathering I had gone to just before I started feeling different and my dreams became so much more lucid. At a gathering in Sedona that I had attended, there was a Peruvian shaman and his assistants whom everyone had come to see. Before the main ceremony, this shaman and I sang some songs together for everyone, and after the ceremony he asked to see me alone briefly before I left.

"That's the one! That's the one!" Xilonen pronounced loudly, without letting me even finish my story. "That's the one that hexed you. He was jealous of you. The people were there to see him, not you. I'm sure he got paid for his services for the ceremony he gave, but he was threatened by you and wanted to make sure you didn't steal his work from him. Well, good; that's finally settled. We took care of that bad wind he sent you; we will deal with him personally later. Right now, we need to begin your instruction and put you on the path."

Just then, there was a knock on the door, and without getting up Xilonen yelled, "Come on in—you're late, as usual."

A few seconds later, a dark-skinned man dressed in full Huichol regalia stepped out onto the patio and blew my mind. It was Alberto, one of the many brothers of Matziwa from the Huichol Sierra. We greeted each other in Huichol and shook hands the special way that Huichol do. But without saying anything else, Alberto asked, "Is he on the path yet?"

Xilonen quickly explained to Alberto all that had happened. Pulling up a chair, he began to tell me about the underworld and the "path" as Xilonen went to get us coffee. "You have been traveling to the underworld, but you cannot direct your path because you do not have the eyes that can see properly there—or, let's say you have the eyes, but they are still closed. What you need to do is find your other, your nagual. Your nagual is an animal spirit that was born in the underworld at the same time you were born, and you and it share the same *tonal*, or soul, even though you live in different worlds. Once you find your nagual, you will be able to navigate in the underworld in your dreams. So tell us, do you have any experience with animals, especially wild ones?"

I began to tell them about the many animals I have had relationships with, and there were so many I think that they both were stunned. Neither of them lived in areas that held so many different species or had traveled as extensively as I had, and I'm guessing some of the animals, birds, and fish I mentioned neither of them had ever seen.

"The Lord of the Animals will like you if you ever meet him," Xilonen said with a laugh when I was finally done listing the animals that I knew. "Okay, let's put it another way," Alberto said with a sigh. "In order to see with an animal in the underworld, two things must happen. You must have a dream with the animal, and you must have a physical part of the animal.

It doesn't matter which happens first. So do you have any parts of any of these animals that you know?"

Again, I began to rattle off a long list of animals whose parts I had obtained either by hunting them, finding them, or them being given to me as gifts. Most were miscellaneous bones or feathers, and others were skulls, hooves, skins, or whole wings or tails.

Xilonen and Alberto looked at each other and both shook their heads and rolled their eyes in mock dismay. Apparently they had expected this to be easier. I guess they hadn't encountered many gringos that possessed such things. Alberto stood up facing me and asked, "Do you have any parts of any of those animals with you here?"

In my hut at Soledad's I had my takwatsi, which I retrieved and brought back to Xilonen's house. In my takwatsi I had muvieris from hawk, vulture, and condor; I also had a piece of deer hide, a small rattle partially filled with cougar teeth, a necklace made from bear claws, a piece of snakeskin, and a raven's foot.

Alberto and Xilonen shook their heads again. After much questioning about how and where I got those animal parts, the two shamans decided it was probably either the deer, condor, or cougar that was my alter ego, my nagual. They also told me that I had such a strong bond with all the animals represented in my takwatsi that once I found my nagual I would be able to turn into any of the animals in my takwatsi to navigate the geography of the underworld most efficiently. It was decided that I was to put my deer hide, condor muvieri, and cougar rattle on the altar by my bed and pray to my nagual to come to me in my dreams that night. Before leaving, Xilonen also told me to have Soledad help me get a little bit of food that each animal liked to eat and put it on the altar as well, in order to entice their spirits in.

The next day, I recounted my dreams to Xilonen and Alberto. Their interpretations of dreams were completely foreign to me. They could each take a simple occurrence and weave a whole tale around it. Since I hadn't actually seen any of the three animals in my dreams, they both interpreted that it was my vantage point during the dreams that was important (I had a dream where I saw a cave, and they both said that was important), which was above the ground, sometimes very high above the ground, and I traveled so far in such little time that I must be a condor. From now on, until I learned to "see" and navigate the underworld, I was to keep the condor feathers by my bed (or wherever I was sleeping) and ritually feed them every day.

To my surprise, Xilonen said that Alberto was going to help me during the next few months with my dreaming. She explained that when I got home, Alberto would be much easier to contact than herself and that he was a master dreamer. Alberto simply smiled as he wrote down his cellphone number for me. He knew I was not surprised at all. He was one of the first Huichol I ever met that legally worked in the United States for a few months out of the year. Through various channels more than ten years ago, Alberto had developed a relationship with the San Diego Zoo to sell his amazing beaded animal figures. While I was living on the East Coast, he came to visit me a few times and to sell his art. We traveled together to many places, and once I even took him to the top of the Empire State Building. For a Huichol he was considered wealthy, and he even owned a pickup truck.

It was decided that I would call Alberto once a week and report to him how I was doing with my dreams. Together, Alberto and Xilonen drew me a crude map of the underworld with the five cardinal directions: "The north is the place of the wind caves and the land of the dead; the east is the sea and holy earth cave; the south is the fire and the caves of heat; the west is the house of the women and the caves of the seven waterfalls; and in the center is the heart with a great plaza, which all else revolves around. You must try and enter from one direction and exit through another; in this way, you will eventually find the center, at which time your training will attain a new level."

Upon returning home, there was a definite shift in my everyday life. It took some time to catch up on the things I had been putting off to get my life back together, but whatever Xilonen had done for me seemed to have worked. It was like before the healing I was carrying a ball and chain that limited me both physically and mentally, but she had cut that chain and now I was free again. Creativity, physicality, curiousness, and a sense of responsibility all flowed through me again.

In terms of my dreams, I began to notice distinctions in perspective at a deeper level. Through keeping a journal of my dreams, I began to notice a pattern of four different perspectives. In the first, I am actively taking part in the dream, either now, in the future, or in the past. The second perspective is harder to describe; I am not aware that I'm participating, nor am I aware that I'm not participating. Third, I experience the dream as though watching a movie; I am aware that I'm dreaming but not participating. Fourth, I dream that I am dreaming, and I wake up in a dream to be in another dream before I actually wake up.

I told Alberto about this before recounting my dreams to him, but he very quickly stated that he was only interested in hearing about the dreams that I knew I was participating in. He also told me to be very careful about dreams within dreams, and that until I was more experienced, if I ever knew I was dreaming within another dream, I was to force myself to wake up because malicious spirits or sorcerers could manipulate my dreams or put me into their dream, and I might never be able to return. Alberto was very clear that what I was to be working on was having an active part in the dreams I was having and to remember them when I awoke. This did not mean total control—just as in everyday life, I had to flow with synchronicities and let things unfold naturally—but to do so with the intent and the discipline to stay on my path. The goal was to dream with such clarity as to be able to bring the dream back with me to the light of everyday consciousness when I woke up. This is how healers use dreams to cure. Without the ability to bring dreams back to the waking world and correctly interpret their meanings, dreams are useless in curing.

During the next three months or so, my dreams transformed from a basically uncontrollable hodgepodge of events, people, and places into a more conscious stream of learning experiences. Very quickly I learned that the underworld, in most cases, reflects the features of our physical world. There are mountains, forests, streams, oceans, animals, highways, and even cities. But there are also places that exist in the underworld that don't exist in the waking world. Alberto called these the enchanted places and was eager that I explore them. Even though I could sometimes return to the same place again in a dream by locating a feature near to where I was before, I found that the geography of the underworld is not static—there are no fixed physical relationships between places as in our physical world.

There are also many different types of spirits or entities inhabiting the underworld. Some live almost full-time in our physical world and manifest as natural forms such as hills, stones, places in water, and animals. Some of these entities can be found in both the underworld and the waking world. These special entities can become helpers, or allies, of shamans, healers, or evil sorcerers, and they also have the ability to punish people as they see fit. They can capture the soul of those doing harm to the natural world or to other living beings. This is one reason shamanic cultures always leave offerings in those places in nature where the underworld and material world meet. In the underworld, bi-local entities that can move between worlds at will often appear as dwarfs. On the other hand, the most powerful beings always appear as larger than human beings and are thought of as "lords." The lords of the underworld have various distinctions and roles; the classification of the underworld entities' social order is complex, and there is no need to go into it here except to say that it is just as complex as the social geography of our waking world.

As in my life in the waking world, I was naturally drawn to the goings-on with nature: trees, plants, bodies of water, mountains, animals, and so on. In the underworld, just as Xilonen predicted, I became a fast student and companion of the Lord of the Animals. Alberto was extremely impressed when I told him this, as he had only met the Lord of the Animals one time. In my relationship with this entity, I began to develop the ability to change at will from a condor to any of my other animal allies, finally realizing that allies from my past such as Ronnie the eagle, the blue deer from Huiricuta, the wolves of the Huichol Sierra, and the spirit of the cougar in Arizona were all bi-local entities that could walk in both the underworld and the waking world. Understanding this explained a lot about the mysteries I had experienced with them. However, as much as I was blown away by that reality, the clincher was one night meeting Itzamna, the dwarf king of Ux-mal. Itzamna gradually became one of my closest allies and friends in the underworld. While I could not transform myself into Itzamna, being able to move around as a condor and change into a deer, cougar, wolf, eagle, hum-mingbird, lizard, mountain goat, or spider was extremely useful in explor-ing the various places of the underworld.

Finally, one day I was flying and came to an enormous square plaza with a castle in the middle, and I knew that I had found the center of the un-derworld. It was a bustling metropolis of both human and animal forms. I immediately turned into my cougar form so I could walk about freely. After exploring many places, I ended up in the castle, and before I knew it I was standing in front of a giant throne. Seated in a huge chair on the throne was a massive man who stared intently at me. I wanted desperately to find out who he was, but something snuck up behind me and attacked me. It was a black jaguar, and everywhere I ran, it would catch up to me. I knew it wanted to eat my soul (tonal). I ran out of the castle and took off as a condor. The jaguar turned into a bird in order to follow me, but it was not a condor and eventually I flew high enough to lose the other bird and was safe. The next morning I called Alberto, and he confirmed that I had found the center of the underworld and that I should go as soon as possible to see Xilonen.

A few weeks later, I was back in Oaxaca, sitting on Xilonen's patio and drinking coffee with her. It took me a full day and most of the night to tell her about my dreams. She would only let me use my journal to begin to re-member a dream, then she would have me tell her about it without reading from the journal. In this way, as my stories unfolded and many hours late into the night, I realized I was telling Xilonen about my dreams in a similar way to how she and Alberto interpreted dreams. Without merely recount-ing the details, I was also using the symbolism of the dreams to weave their stories into the light of waking reality.

Xilonen was very pleased with my progress but said that I needed to confront for myself the evil wind that still pursued me. "The evil wind sent to you by that Peruvian sorcerer—I scared it away here, but now that you are traveling in the underworld, you need to take care of it there and also confront the sorcerer who cast it upon you. He is the one on the throne you saw in your dream. He deceived you. There is no king in the underworld and especially no one man. The highest lords are of both sexes, male and female, and none of them sit on any damn throne! He appeared that way to scare you, and the jaguar that attacked you is his evil wind."

It took me more than a week under the guidance of Xilonen to finally be rid of the Peruvian sorcerer. In the end, I had fought with and eaten all of his animal allies except the cobra, and while trying to escape me I chased him into a pack of mongooses, who took quick care of him. I don't know what happened to him in the waking world, but he and his evil wind never bothered me again.

Knowing that I would probably be staying in Oaxaca for a while, I arranged things at home, and over the next two months Xilonen had me participate as an apprentice in her almost-daily healing sessions. I was amazed at how far some people came to see her. Typically she would meet with a patient (and his or her family) with me quietly observing, and then that night we would dream for the patient. The next day, she would compare the interpretations of my dreams against hers. It was fascinating to see both the similarities and the differences. I had brought almost all of my animal spirits with me in my takwatsi, and one night Xilonen brought out her secret case and showed me hers but with the promise I would tell no one what was inside. Even though Xilonen always used her own interpretation of her dreams to heal her clients, she gradually had me assist her in the actual healing ceremony done for the client a day or two later in a similar way to the ceremony she did for me. However, Xilonen was quite clear that she would not show me how to fold and cut the effigies she used. They came directly from her ancestors and would be of no use to me. I would have to find my own manner of trapping the evil winds of my clients once I began to cure people on my own.

Although I was admittedly disappointed that Xilonen would not share that aspect of her craft with me, and I was confused and skeptical about how I would find my own way, it all happened quite naturally when I was visiting the city of Oaxaca a few weeks later with Armando.

We had been in the city staying with one of Armando's sisters and planned to leave the next morning. We had purchased many things for Armando's family and some of the other people of his village that could only be found in the city, and both of us were anxious to get back. That evening, we were waiting for Armando's sister Maria to come home from work, but when she arrived she had two Americans with her. Right away it was apparent that they were husband and wife, and judging from their clothes they were well-to-do financially. Maria began to explain that their daughter was sick and needed help. I wasn't sure what I could do, but I offered to speak with them.

Their daughter Kate had been away at a highly respected boarding school that she had attended for two years. But this time, upon returning home for the summer, she was markedly different. The once happy, mischievous, and outgoing Kate was now but a shell of her former self. They told me she barely ate and had lost considerable weight, and she did not want to go anywhere or speak with people, including them. They had taken her to doctors and they had found nothing physically wrong with her, and she had been seen by counselors, but Kate would not open up to them. The couple had heard that I was trained in native folk healing and asked for my help.

Taking Armando and Maria aside, I frankly told them that I had never attempted to cure anyone in the manner they were suggesting—that I was only a helper to Xilonen, but of course Armando already knew that. I knew that there were experienced healers in Oaxaca and told Maria that she should take the girl to one of them. However, Maria said she already had taken the couple to see two curanderos, and the couple did not feel comfortable with them. Maria insisted that since I was from their culture, it would be easier for them to accept what I was doing, and also that Kate would understand because she only spoke a little Spanish and that the other healers did not speak English well enough. We discussed the matter at length, with me countering all of Maria's points that I was the one to do it, when Armando finally stepped in. He put a hand on one of my shoulders, as is his people's custom when saying something important, and very clearly told me that from all he knew of the situation, "it was my time"—that these people were brought to me and I could not refuse them, and that this is the way it worked for healers. This girl did not have a medical situation but a spiritual/heart condition. This is what I had been training for; to turn them away would be a disgrace to Xilonen, Alberto, my nagual and allies, and the lords of the underworld. As my last line of defense, I suggested that we take them to see Xilonen, and I would assist her. But almost triumphantly Maria stated that the family was leaving Mexico in two days, so there would not be time. I finally agreed.

I went out to the car where Kate was waiting and explained to her who I was and that I had been asked to help her. I did not ask her permission, for if she refused I could not force her. My strategy was to get her interested in her own healing. I took off my rose-bead necklace and gently put it around her neck while explaining to her that it was powerful medicine and something very special to me. It would help her sleep that night, and she could give it back to me tomorrow. I asked her if she had anything of hers that might help me through the night, and she immediately shook her head no. I knew I had to have something of hers for my dreaming, but I didn't want to press her. I would have to try to get something of hers from her parents. But then Kate surprised the heck out of me. Just as I was about to shut the car door, she said "Wait!" as she reached into her purse and pulled out a pin. "This is a pin from my school that all the girls wear. You can have it—I don't want it anymore. I'm not going back there."

Taking the pin, I said goodnight to Kate and told her I would see her tomorrow. Just before closing the car door, I noticed a look of relief on Kate's face and that with her left hand she was touching my beads. Somehow those two things renewed my confidence that maybe I could actually help her. As I walked up the front steps to the house, the pin suddenly felt extremely heavy in my hand, and I knew for sure that something terrible had happened at that school.

Armando and Maria had already given the parents a list of things to purchase for the ceremony the next day. I looked over the list of usual offerings and added a few more items: five more special candles and any photos they had of Kate and of her boarding school and any people she went to school with there.

Even though they were not formally trained as curanderos, Armando and Maria were both pretty much experts at the ceremonial aspect of the healing rituals conducted by Xilonen and other dreamers, since they had been participating in them their whole lives. They were a huge help in preparing me for my night of dreams and for the healing ceremony the next day. Talking everything out at dinner put me much more at ease, and together we said many prayers at Maria's altar before going to bed.

Itzamna was waiting for me as I flew in the east entrance of the underworld, and I explained to him what was going on. While I was talking with Itzamna on the beach, my wolves came, and then Ronnie, and finally the blue deer. The spirit animals were quiet but restless, as if they already knew there was work to be done. I showed them the pin and asked them to find me the school; I figured that was the best place to start. While they were gone, Itzamna and I discussed what to do once we found it.

"Itzamna, if we can find the school, could you go there in the physical world and check it out?" I asked, not knowing if that was possible.

"Sure, I and Ronnie and the wolves and the blue deer can travel wherever we want. The only question is, what are we looking for? There might not even be anyone there, and even if there is, what can we do?"

Just then Ronnie came back. The wolves had found the school, and Ronnie had already gone through the veil and checked out the school in the physical dimension. There were no students or teachers around, only a few caretakers, but Ronnie did have a bad feeling while flying around one section of offices. The blue deer and the wolves returned. I didn't know what to do and felt totally useless. With that thought, a giant wave crashed into me and all went black.

My next dream was with the Lord of the Animals. I remember I actually laughed to myself in my dream because although the Lord of Animals appeared to me in many different forms, this time, the most serious time yet, he appeared as a mythological figure: a centaur.

"You have treated me and my children with respect," the Lord Centaur said in a very serious voice. "I have heard you need help in curing an innocent little girl. Since you now are beginning to walk the good path, I will give you a hint to get you started on your journey: do you know that the little girl's nagual lives here with me?"

That was it! Whatever happened to the little girl's tonal would have happened to her nagual, as we all share the same tonal with our nagual.

From the energy of the pin, my wolves had already found the nagual of the little girl, hiding in a small crack of a tall cliff, and I had Ronnie go get her. She was a frail-looking little swallow that was frightened by all of us except the blue deer. The blue deer found out from her that she was hiding from an evil man who made her do nasty things to him. She was very ashamed of what he would make her do, but that was all she would say. The Lord of the Animals, however, did have one more thing to say. "Many of my children are hurt or sick; if you help this little one, I will return the favor."

Itzamna helped me up from where I was lying on the beach. Somehow I just knew he had sent that wave at me. "This evil man obviously likes little girls, and this is how you will capture his evil wind..."

When I woke up, I immediately called Kate's parents and asked them if they had found any photos from Kate's school. Her mother told me that Kate had a yearbook and that they would bring it. "Perfect!" I heard a little voice say. I couldn't see him, but I knew Itzamna was there. I just wished I had as much confidence as Itzamna that everything actually was perfect.

Since Kate and her parents had no family in Oaxaca, I asked Maria to invite some trusted friends and any of their kids to come over for the ceremony and to bring any musical instruments they might have, especially hand drums or rattles. To my delight, the half-dozen friends and their children were all native to Oaxaca and familiar with this type of healing ceremony. They even brought food and drinks with them, along with beautiful drums and rattles.

When Kate and her parents arrived, I asked the parents to help out in the kitchen so I could have Kate to myself. Together, we dressed up the altar with all the things they had brought. I turned the whole process into a game. Kate did not laugh or really play, but she did participate in the whole process and even became more enthusiastic when she found out that everything we were doing was for her. Just before we were done dressing the altar, I casually—and not looking at her—told Kate that I knew a man at her school had made her do bad things, but that she never had to see him again and that he would be punished for what he did and never hurt any other little girls. She looked up into my eyes, and I could tell that she truly wanted to believe me but also still had doubts. She was feeling overwhelmed by trying to process how in the world I could know about her experiences with the man, and at the same time she was at the center of an ancient and extremely complex healing ceremony.

With all the preparations made, everyone gathered in the living room where the altar was, and I asked for the drumming and rattling to begin and for the copal smoke to be distributed. This was more for Kate than anyone else. I wanted to keep her rational mind as far off from what we were doing as possible, and I made sure she had a rattle as well, which she gladly accepted from Maria. I also placed a garland of fresh flowers around Kate's neck and asked her to help me light all the candles on the altar and around the room. While she was doing that, I chanted the names of my spirit helpers that walk in both worlds and lit the five candles at the base of the altar: one each for Itzamna, Kumukemay (wolves), Ocelotl (cougar), Kahullumari (blue deer), and Ronnie (eagle). Though I could not see them, their now well-known feeling pervaded the room, and I knew they were there.

With Kate now standing beside me in front of the altar, I quietly asked her to focus on the light of the five candles on the floor as I chanted for her in the way Xilonen had taught me, but this time in English. This form of ritual chanting incorporates the maladies of the patient but always names the offending spirits, the maladies, the offerings, and then the pleads or demands that the afflictions of the patient be removed. This is chanted in sets of five (with usually between 50 and 200 chants in total) to speak for the sick one.

Here is what I chanted:

Hear me, diseased winds blowing
Hear me, disease flowing from the place of the dead
Hear me, disease of disrespect toward our mother (earth)
Hear me, disease of gossip among people
Hear me, disease of hurt against others

You take the essence of the good heart and replace it
With sickness
With fever
With pain
With depression

You take our thirst
You take our hunger
You take our blood
But the strength of our mother pervades
The light of our father shines through

Where this girl walks
Where she works
In her house
With her family
With her classmates

With the help of the spirits, this affliction will end
This fever
These pains
These thoughts
These shames

Lords of the Underworld, we honor you
With sacred flesh
With sacred shells
With sacred cactus
With sacred tobacco

So that henceforth
Where she goes walking
Where she goes praying
Where she goes sleeping
Where she goes talking

Malicious spirits do not interfere!
To reclaim strength
To reclaim wisdom
To reclaim health
To reclaim soul

She has been given good memory
She has been given good heart
She has been given pure womb
She has been given good vision
She has been given good life

She will go walking in beauty
She will go working in beauty
She will go talking in beauty
Mother God, so shall it be
Father God, so shall it be

I then asked that everyone place the food and other offerings to the spirits next to the five spirit-candles on the floor. While they were doing this, I took the yearbook from the altar and quietly chanted to my spirit helpers and Mother-Father God to help me. As I opened the book, a wind entered the room (it felt like Itzamna) and rapidly turned the pages until it got to a page of school administrators, and I saw the man's face. I pointed to it, and Kate nodded her head yes. She did not seem fearful at all but stared up at me with awe that I knew.

Gently, I laid her down on the floor and used the sucking technique of the Huichol healers on her, an ancient healing practice that I had been taught by Nichu many years before. I instructed Kate to watch me carefully, and when I breathed in, she was to breathe out; when I breathed out, she was to breathe in. Drawing in my breath and then rapidly exhaling at her forehead, eyes, solar plexus, hands, navel, and feet, I sucked out and expelled the evil winds from Kate's body, mind, and soul. (If Kate were an adult, I would have asked her to relive in her mind those experiences she wanted to get rid of while performing this part of the healing, but in this case, seeing the photo of the man was enough.) With that evil energy now gone, I replaced it with energy of the fire, water, air, and earth by first blowing smoke into the nine places I had sucked and then by gently rubbing soil and water onto her whole body. (Since Kate was obviously the victim of sexual abuse, I conducted this part as superficially as possible, without losing the essence of the procedure.)

Helping Kate stand up, I saw tears in her eyes, but she was being very brave and did not cry or complain. I took the yearbook and asked for more drumming and rattling. Placing the yearbook on the floor, open to the page of the man, I lit one last candle and told Kate to place it over his face. I quietly explained to Kate that the five candles represented my helpers, that they were there with us in the room and that we were going to ask them for help.

Armando, Maria, and her friends all knew what I was going to do, and they followed my lead. I called each spirit and asked them to look out for Kate, to protect her and give her light and strength. After enumerating out loud the qualities of each spirit, I had Kate blow out each candle and with her hands move the smoke onto her, therefore putting some of their spirit into her. While I enumerated each spirit's qualities and how they would help Kate, the rest of the group repeated them with me, and by the second candle, Kate and her parents were doing it too, and as we went, the louder and stronger the whole ceremony became.

Finished with the five candles, I moved to the last one on the floor that was sitting on the picture in the yearbook. I placed Kate's pin next to the candle and invoked the evil wind of the man into the candle. The group continued following my single chants and repeating them after me:

> *You have no power here!*
> *You have no power over Kate!*
> *She is stronger than you now!*
> *She has powerful protectors.*
> *You will never hurt her again!*
>
> *Kate is free from you!*
> *Get out of here, you coward!*
> *Get out of here, you evil wind!*
> *This we command you!*
> *This we demand of you!*

I told Kate to blow out the candle with all her might and then step away from the smoke as the evil man's wind blew away and dissipated. In total silence, Kate stared into the candle and then blew it out. She stepped back and watched the smoke for a moment, and then turned and jumped into her parents' arms. Everyone clapped and cheered. To my delight, Kate turned to me and took off my necklace. "I don't need this anymore," she said. And as she handed it back to me, our eyes met and I could clearly see that she was going to be much better now, and tears came to my eyes.

To my utter surprise, from the shadows of the back of the room, Xilonen stepped out. "It seems we have a new healer. Welcome to the path, mighty condor."

Epilogue

I never saw Kate or her family again, but I gave them my cell-phone number and a few months later received a call from her father saying that she was doing well, even though she was changed. She still harbored a fear of certain adult men, but not all. And from what I gathered, even though she did play, in general she acted much more mature than her friends and classmates, which I thought was perfectly normal.

The one thing he said that put the biggest smile on my face was that Kate would ask her parents at times to light a candle for her, and she would simply sit there and watch it for a while before she blew it out. But I already knew this. Since they had returned to the United States, I had gone and found Kate's nagual, the little swallow, in the underworld several times. The little swallow would play with the others but she acted more like the leader, and I knew one day she would grow up to be a leader. While speaking with the swallow, she asked me how she could find me if she needed me or wanted to talk. I told her all she had to do was fly to a place where there were candles burning and call me through the flame, and I would come as soon as possible—which, at times, she did.

I never asked the parents about the man at the school, and they didn't say anything about it to me. However, while talking with the father, I intuitively sensed from his voice that the man had one way or another been brought to justice.

As for me, I have outlived most of my teachers in this book but still keep in touch with a few, including Maggie, Xilonen, Kani, the Huichol, and of course with my usher, Amy. I continued with my dreaming and healing work but also began healing others by reconnecting them with nature through my workshops and guiding service, and of course I continue to write.

Then one day, while visiting Mexico, I ended up in the state of Veracruz and went to the Congreso Internacional de Brujeria (International Conference of Witchcraft) in Catemaco with some friends. It was there that I was swept up into yet another realm of shamanism, and I have spent many years since then learning from the "witches" in the remote Tuxtlas Mountains. But that is another story...

COMING IN DECEMBER 2011 FROM
James Endredy

The Flying Witches of Veracruz

A Shaman's True Story of Indigenous Witchcraft,
Devil's Weed, and Trance Healing in Aztec Brujeria

WWW.LLEWELLYN.COM

GET MORE AT LLEWELLYN.COM

Visit us online to browse hundreds of our books and decks, plus sign up to receive our e-newsletters and exclusive online offers.

- Free tarot readings • Spell-a-Day • Moon phases
- Recipes, spells, and tips • Blogs • Encyclopedia
- Author interviews, articles, and upcoming events

GET SOCIAL WITH LLEWELLYN

Find us on Facebook

www.Facebook.com/LlewellynBooks

Follow us on

twitter

www.Twitter.com/Llewellynbooks

GET BOOKS AT LLEWELLYN

LLEWELLYN ORDERING INFORMATION

Order online: Visit our website at www.llewellyn.com to select your books and place an order on our secure server.

Order by phone:
- Call toll free within the U.S. at 1-877-NEW-WRLD (1-877-639-9753)
- Call toll free within Canada at 1-866-NEW-WRLD (1-866-639-9753)
- We accept VISA, MasterCard, and American Express

Order by mail:
Send the full price of your order (MN residents add 6.875% sales tax) in U.S. funds, plus postage and handling to: Llewellyn Worldwide, 2143 Wooddale Drive, Woodbury, MN 55125-2989

POSTAGE AND HANDLING:
STANDARD (U.S., Mexico & Canada)
(Please allow 2 business days):
$25.00 and under, add $4.00.
$25.01 and over, FREE SHIPPING.

INTERNATIONAL ORDERS
(airmail only):
$16.00 for one book, plus $3.00 for each additional book.

Visit us online for more shipping options.

Prices subject to change.

FREE CATALOG!

To order, call
1-877-NEW-WRLD
ext. 8236
or visit our website

ECOSHAMANISM

Sacred
Practices
of
Unity,
Power
&
Earth
Healing

JAMES ENDREDY

Ecoshamanism

Sacred Practices of Unity, Power and Earth Healing

JAMES ENDREDY

In a society riddled with rampant consumerism and unsustainable technology, it's easy for everyone, including shamans, to lose touch with the natural world. James Endredy, who has learned from tribal shamans around the globe, presents a new philosophy of shamanic practice called ecological shamanism, or ecoshamanism. Designed to deliver well-being and spiritual harmony, ecoshamanism is the culmination of the visionary practices, rituals, and ceremonies that honor and support nature.

Exploring the holistic perspective of shamanism, Endredy encourages readers to establish a rewarding connection with sacred, life-giving forces using shamanic tools and practices. The author describes more than fifty authentic ecoshamanistic practices—including ceremonies, rituals, chanting, hunting, pilgrimage, and making instruments—that reinforce one's relationship with the natural world.

0-7387-0742-6, 360 pp, 7¹/₂ x 9¹/₈ $19.95

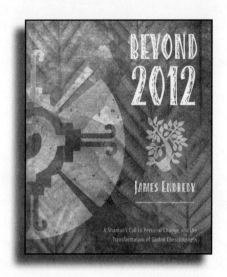

BEYOND
2012

JAMES ENDREDY

A Shaman's Call to Personal Change and the
Transformation of Global Consciousness

Beyond 2012

A Shaman's Call to Personal Change and the Transformation of Global Consciousness

JAMES ENDREDY

War, catastrophic geologic events, Armageddon … the prophecies surrounding 2012—the end of the Mayan calendar—aren't pretty. James Endredy pierces the doom and gloom with hope and a positive, hopeful message for humankind.

For wisdom and guidance concerning this significant date, Endredy consults Tataiwari (Grandfather Fire) and Nakawe (Grandmother Growth)—the "First Shamans." Recorded here is their fascinating dialog. They reveal how the evolution of human consciousness, sustaining the earth, and our personal happiness are all interconnected.

Discover what you can do to spur the transformation of human consciousness. See how connecting with our true selves, daily acts of compassion and love, focusing personal energy, and even gardening can make a difference. Endredy also shares shamanistic techniques to revive the health of our planet … and ourselves.

978-0-7387-1158-4, 240 pp, 7¹/₂ x 9¹/₈ $16.95

Shamanism

For Beginners

Walking with the World's Healers
of Earth and Sky

JAMES ENDREDY

Shamanism for Beginners
Walking with the World's Healers of Earth and Sky

JAMES ENDREDY

Interest in shamanism is on the rise, and people are eager to integrate this intriguing tradition into their own lives. *Shamanism for Beginners* introduces the spiritual beliefs and customs of the shaman—a spiritual leader, visionary, healer, diviner, walker between worlds, and so much more.

How is one called to be a shaman? How is a shaman initiated? Where does a shaman's power come from? Exploring the practices and beliefs of tribes around the world, James Endredy sheds light on the entire shamanic experience. The fascinating origins and evolution of shamanism are examined, along with power places, tools (costume, drum, sweat lodge, medicine wheel), sacred plants, and the relationship between the shaman and spirits. Enriched with the author's personal stories and quotes from actual shaman elders and scholars, Endredy concludes with incredible feats of shamans, healing techniques, and ruminations on the future of this remarkable tradition.

978-0-7387-1562-9, 288 pp, 5³/₁₆ x 8 $14.95

To Write to the Author

If you wish to contact the author or would like more information about this book, please write to the author in care of Llewellyn Worldwide, and we will forward your request. Both the author and the publisher appreciate hearing from you and learning of your enjoyment of this book and how it has helped you. Llewellyn Worldwide cannot guarantee that every letter written to the author will be answered, but all will be forwarded. Please write to:

James Endredy
c/o Llewellyn Worldwide
2143 Wooddale Drive
Woodbury, MN 55125-2989
Please enclose a self-addressed stamped envelope for reply,
or $1.00 to cover costs. If outside U.S.A., enclose
international postal reply coupon.

Many of Llewellyn's authors have websites with additional information and resources. For more information, please visit our website:

HTTP://WWW.LLEWELLYN.COM

Journey into the Exhilarating, Bizarre, Brutal, and Humorous Realm of the Shaman

Join James Endredy, noted author and shamanic practitioner, on an incredible excursion into realities that few people have had a chance to explore. Whether it's discovering how to dream with the Lords of the Underworld or learning to fly with the help of his eagle *nagual*, outwitting a soul-stealing sorceress in Veracruz or conversing with the spirit of an ancient dwarf king, these gripping firsthand accounts chronicle Endredy's mystical experiences while living and working with fifteen indigenous cultures in North and South America, Hawaii, and Mexico.

Endredy's amazing, arduous, and sometimes life-threatening initiations and lessons illustrate the interconnectedness of all life, the importance of being humble enough to laugh at yourself, and the need to respect and learn from nature and her children.

James Endredy (Arizona) has devoted more than twenty-five years to studying and participating in shamanic practices. He is the author of *Ecoshamanism, Shamanism for Beginners,* and *Beyond 2012;* has presented at the International Conference on Shamanism; and has appeared on the History Channel. Visit him at www.jamesendredy.com.

Llewellyn Worldwide
www.llewellyn.com
www.facebook.com/LlewellynBooks

$16.95 US
$19.50 CAN

ISBN 978-0-7387-2147-7